FOOD - & - WELLNESS

THE SOBELL HOUSE VEGETARIAN COOK BOOK

Foreword by Amelia Foster, CEO Sobell House

Welcome to our second cookbook: Food & Wellness, The Sobell House Vegetarian Cookbook.

I am honoured to have been asked to write this foreword nearly a year after joining Sobell House Hospice Charity as CEO. Every day I work here feels like an enormous privilege, raising funds as we do to support the amazing and compassionate work of our hospice and community teams. Indeed, this year has seen the launch of our Home Hospice Care Team, co-funded with Macmillan Cancer Support and Social Finance, enabling us to care for those who wish to die at home and helping to support their loved ones so they can make the most of the time they have left. Without the support of people like you, we could not develop and maintain such important services, which help people live well until they die.

Part of living well is eating well, and being able to share meals with friends and family. Sobell House Hospice is a place of hospitality as well as healthcare, and it is fabulous to be able to share a recipe from Paul, one of our chefs. By eating vegan and vegetarian meals and therefore less meat, we can reduce our own carbon footprint (helping us all to live well) and meet our daily target of five portions of fruit and vegetables, as recommended by the NHS. Having read through the recipes in this book – many of them from wonderful Oxfordshire restaurants – I am excited to be giving them a go, though as a vegetarian I was always going to love this book. I sincerely hope you do too; it will help us raise vital funds, as well as helping us help the planet. What a win-win!

No foreword would be complete without thanking the incredible people who have been part of creating this book. We have been able to bring you this, our second cookbook, due to the incredibly generous sponsorship of IP Asset Partnership and Oxford Economics, and the expertise of the team at Meze Publishing. We continue to be grateful to our Charity Ambassador Paul Chahidi who supports us with his valuable time and delicious recipes, and we are also delighted to have contributions from Rick Stein, Florence Pugh, Mel Giedroyc, Matt Allwright, Roger Allam and Huw Edwards. inally, we are honoured to have recipes from Victoria Bradley, our Clinical Lead, and Mary Miller, the End of Life Lead within the Oxfordshire Hospitals. We thank them for their commitment to end of life and palliative care, leading the way in making Sobell House Hospice such a special place.

I hope you enjoy exploring the vegetarian and vegan delights within!

MISS C. TAYLOR
NURSING ASSISTANT
NHS
Oxford University Hospitals
NHS Foundation Trust
Farhiya Abdi
Senior Nursing Assistant
SOBELL

Contents

Editorial

Foreword
Amelia Foster, Chief Executive 2

Introduction
Sobell House: Where Wellbeing Matters 6
Foodie Fundraising Ideas 10
Directory 124

Guest Recipes

Florence Pugh
Tzatziki 30
Huw Edwards
Burrata with Broad Bean and Almond Pesto 44
Matt Allwright
Mean and Moody Chilli Jam 58
Mel Giedroyc
Ellen's Gorgeous Gluten-Free Pizza Wraps 72
Paul Chahidi
Akilima's Epic Bengali Dhal 86
Rick Stein
Whole Eggs in Coconut Masala 100
Roger Allam
Peperonata 110

Sobell House Recipes
Mary Miller
Aubergine Rolls 12
Paul Allday
Roasted Sweet Potato and Tofu Stew 14
Dr Victoria Bradley
Queen of Puddings 16

Recipes from friends of Sobell House
Acropolis Greek Taverna
The Great Taste of the Mediterranean 18
Gemista (Stuffed Vegetables) 20
The Alice at The Randolph Hotel
Down the Rabbit Hole 22
Mushroom Risotto 24
Bhoomi Kitchen
Business is Bhooming! 26
Aloo Bonda 28
Café Coco, Kazbar and Café Tarifa
Creating Culinary Magic 32
Vegan Burger 34
The Eyston Arms
Welcomed with Open Arms 36
Rhubarb, Pistachio and Orange Tart 38
The Gardeners Arms
Good Food and Green Thumbs 40
Vegan Chicken Caesar Style Salad 42

Jolly Good Brownies

Time To Treat Yourself 46

Baileys Coffee and Chocolate Cake 48

The Old Bookbinders

Old Stories are the Best 50

Le Cassoulet Méditerranéen 52

Oxford Fine Dining

The Finest Catering for Every Eventuality 54

Lentil Dhal with Kachumber Salad 56

Parsonage Grill

Sunday Roasts Have a New Look 60

Roast Cauliflower with Pistachio & Capers 62

The Picnic Hamper

Good Honest Cooking 64

Falafel with Salad and Pitta 66

Pierre Victoire

Bon Appétit! 68

Tartiflette du Maison 70

Pindy's Samosas

Homemade and From the Heart 74

Butternut Squash Sabji 76

The Plough at Hanney

Breaking New Ground 78

Plough Bhaji Burger 80

The Secret Supper Society

Be Our Guest 82

Pasta Pie 84

Studley Wood Golf Club

Breakfast, Lunch and Tee 88

Zingy Lentil and Halloumi Salad 90

Taste Tibet

Happy Everest After... 92

Mixed Vegetable Creamy Coconut Curry 94

The Tite Inn

A Source of Inspiration 96

Ratatouille Risotto with Rocket Pesto 98

The White Hart

Hospitality at Hart 102

Stuffed Tempura Courgette Flower with Summer Veg 104

The White Hart of Wytham

An English Idyll 106

Roasted Red Pepper Gnocchi, Smoked Garlic & Basil Espuma, Parmesan Crisp 108

White Rabbit

Italian Food with a Twist 112

The Rainbow Vegan Pizza 114

Worton Kitchen Garden

From Farm to Fork 116

Nasu Dengaku 118

The Yurt at Nicholsons

Dining with the Best Intentions 120

Twice Baked Cheese Soufflé with Granny Smith Apple, Toasted Hazelnut and Watercress Salad 122

Sobell House:
Where Wellbeing Matters

Sobell House has been providing compassionate care at the heart of its community since 1976. All those years ago, local people coming together to raise vital funds, alongside the NHS, Sir Michael Sobell and the NSCR enabled a much-needed palliative care service in Oxfordshire to be established: Sobell House. Today, throughout the hospice, the wellbeing of our patients, their loved ones, and our staff continue to be of utmost importance. Our aim in all that we do is to create an environment that feels like a home, through the serenity of our gardens, the tastiness of our home cooked food, and the warmth and kindness of our staff.

The hospice is now jointly funded by the NHS and Sobell House Hospice Charity. We see the kindness of our community coming together to support our mission to enrich the lives of our patients and those who love and care for them. Every person is seen as an individual, each with their own unique needs; whether these are physical, psychological, social or spiritual, we seek to come alongside those in our care in order to enable them to live life in the way they desire in their final days. Both the bigger decisions, like deciding on the specifics of medical care, as well as the smaller decisions about which of their favourite meals they would like our resident chef to make for them, all play a significant part in caring for each person.

Alan shares the experience he and his wife, Tracey, had of Sobell when Tracey spent her last days on the inpatient ward: "What was clear to me is that none of the staff at Sobell House see working there as just a job, for them it is so much more than that. Nothing whatsoever was too much trouble for them and being under their care was such a relief. One moment really sticks in my mind, which was when a staff member massaged Tracey's feet. A very simple act of care and kindness, but it meant a lot to us. Tracey and I grew up in Oxford and I've always known about Sobell House and what they do, as other members of our family have been cared for by them over the years. My first impression back then remains the same today – they care for people with such kindness, and provide that same level of care and support to the whole family too."

SOBELL
HOUSE
If the door does not open automatically, please use bell. A member of staff will respond as soon as possible
Automatic door
Automatic door

Sobell House: Where Wellbeing Matters

Our care also extends outside the walls of the hospice building, where our Community Team visit those with life-limiting illness in their homes or an outpatient clinic. In all they do, our specially trained team focus on enabling quality of life, and what that means for each person, taking into account their wishes for how they would like to live and what aspects of our care they would like to access. Working in collaboration with the clinical team, the charity, which raises around £2m from our community in funding each year, seeks to enhance the kind and compassionate care that our patients receive by continuing to develop various services to further support the wellbeing of both inpatients and outpatients.

Our Living Well Centre, Transport Services, Music and Art Therapies and our Catering Service all provide those who come to Sobell with a range of opportunities to live as well and as fully as they can in the time they have left. In addition, our Bereavement Service offers a safe space for those who have lost a loved one to receive supportive counselling following a loss. All of these services, just like the medical care, focus on meeting the needs of our patients, and are delivered with kindness, sensitivity, professionalism and compassion, making a difference to the lives of those who are impacted by the hospice.

John benefitted from visiting our Day Centre (now the Living Well service), supported by our Transport service. Sarah, John's mum, and Zoe, John's wife, share the impact the hospice had on him:

"By this time, John was nearly blind and needed to have someone with him all the time, but the Day Centre was a place where he could still be relatively independent. John was also very sociable and one of the worst things for him was the restriction in his social life caused by his blindness. Sobell were able to provide him with some sense of going out and meeting people, including the drivers who picked him up and dropped him off. He was very pleased when he brought back garlic bread that he'd made at the Day Centre – he was happy to be able to help me make dinner again. They did question whether the amount of garlic he'd put on was due to him not being able to see at all by that point – but he was correct in telling them we just loved lots of garlic!"

The services funded by the charity and the expert medical care provided by the clinical teams combine to create a holistic approach where the wellbeing of our patients and their loved ones is central to the work of this very special place.

SOBELL HOUSE
for Oxfordshire
OXFORD HALF

Foodie Fundraising Ideas
Let's get creative in the kitchen!

The care at Sobell House is only possible because of the kindness and generosity of our supporters. We do hope our wonderful cookbook will encourage you to get creative in the kitchen and come together with friends, family or colleagues to raise much needed funds to support Sobell House. There is nothing more fun or tasty than a Foodie Fundraiser! Here are a few ideas to give you some inspiration.

Host A 'School Dinner' Night

Host a dinner party with a side of nostalgia by taking inspiration from the school dinners of your childhood. Use your favourite dishes from your school days as a starting point for your own twist on traditional dishes and ask everyone to donate at the door.

Mince Pie Monday

How about taking part in Sobell House's very own Mince Pie Monday, held annually on the second Monday in December. This wonderful day gives you the perfect opportunity to have fun with friends, family, and colleagues and get into the Christmas spirit... and it's a great excuse to eat as many mince pies as you like!

Bake Sale

All of us love a good cake stall. How about asking friends to bake lovely cakes, scones, muffins... the options are endless. All you need then is a table to put them on and a place to sell them!

BBQ Party & Cook Off

Get some drinks, some burgers and enjoy the glorious British weather with a community-wide barbecue! Ask your guests to donate and get to know your neighbours a bit better. You can even hold a cook-off and award prizes for the best dishes.

Chocolate Party

Set up a chocolate party in your community! Get cafés, pastry shops, and local chefs to donate their most chocolatey creations in exchange for free advertising. Sell tickets at the door and hold a celebration of this delicious treat for a good cause

Bring a Dish Party

Ask guests to bring a dish and sell recipes or charge admission. It's a great excuse to enjoy a relaxed evening while enjoying the culinary skills of your guests.

Rise and Shine Pancake Breakfast

Fancy an early morning fundraising event? This fun event has participants paying an entrance fee for all-you-can-eat pancakes. It usually includes pancakes, syrup, fruit, eggs and sausages, coffee and juice... all your favourite breakfast foods! Invite your friends, family and neighbours for an early morning fundraiser!

Cooking with Class

We are always looking to improve our cooking skills. With a cooking class fundraiser, people can learn to cook new things while giving to a good cause. Find a local chef to donate their time and share their expertise. Sell tickets to the event and once the class is over, the participants get to enjoy the food they prepared. Great fun!

Come Dine with Me

You will have seen it on the television, but how about arranging your very own Come Dine with Me? It could be Mum v. Dad or kids v. parents, or even grandparents, neighbours and work colleagues! Each person takes a turn to cook and entertain everyone, throughout the week or over the course of the month. Each participant scores the host out of a possible 10 points and the winner is revealed at the end. Agree an entry fee for your guests to fundraise throughout the competition!

Safari Supper

A safari supper is a sociable and fun way to raise money for your group. It takes the form of a dinner party in which each successive course is prepared and eaten at the residence of a different host.

If you would like to know more about foodie fundraising, please call **01865 857007** or email **mail@sobellhospice.org** – we would love to hear from you.

Dr Mary Miller, Consultant in Palliative Medicine at Sobell House

Aubergine Rolls

This recipe makes a regular appearance at important family events. I first made this dish for my wedding and it was ideal. It started as a warm dish and those who had been delayed by storms finished it off cold. It also has the enormous advantage of never going wrong!

Preparation time: 20 minutes, plus cooling | Cooking time: 35 minutes | Makes 12 rolls

2 large aubergines
3 lemons, juiced
105ml olive oil
100ml balsamic vinegar
150ml water
2 cloves of garlic, crushed
1 small red chilli, deseeded and finely chopped
2 tsp mustard seeds
2 tsp cumin seeds
1 tsp five spice powder
100ml maple syrup
100g dried apricots, roughly chopped
50g pine nuts
150g feta cubes
20 mint leaves, roughly chopped

Preheat the oven to 180°c fan. Cut 12 thin slices lengthways from the aubergines and dice the remainder. Place the slices in a shallow tray, then pour over the juice of 2 lemons and 30ml of the olive oil. Cook in the oven for 15 minutes so the aubergine slices are soft but not browned.

Heat 15ml of the olive oil in a saucepan and fry the diced aubergine for 2 minutes. Add the balsamic vinegar, water, garlic, red chilli, mustard seeds, cumin seeds, five spice powder, maple syrup, dried apricots and the pine nuts. Bring the contents to the boil, then reduce and simmer with the lid on for 10 minutes. After the 10 minutes, remove the lid and simmer for a further 5 minutes. Take the saucepan off the heat and allow the chutney to cool.

Once cooled, add the feta cubes to a third of the chutney.

Lay the aubergine slices on a flat surface and spoon the chutney and feta mix equally onto each slice, and then roll up. Place them on a large flat serving plate.

With the remaining two thirds of the chutney, add the final 60ml of olive oil, juice of the last lemon and the roughly chopped mint leaves, then scatter the mixture over the rolls. Serve warm or cold with fresh baguette slices and green salad.

From Raymond Blanc, Blanc Vite 1998. ISBN 0 7472 1708 4

Paul Allday, Sobell House Hospice Chef

Roasted Sweet Potato and Tofu Stew

A few years ago, when training for the cycling world championships, after some research I decided to put myself on a vegetarian diet, which proved to really help my wellbeing and strength. This recipe became one of my favourites and is a very filling, hearty dish that I really enjoyed in the winter months after getting home from long, cold training rides with my GB team mates.

Preparation time: 20 minutes | Cooking time: 30-45 minutes | Serves: 4

2 sweet potatoes
250g smoked tofu
1 shallot
2 cloves of garlic
1 red chilli
1 lime
½ tsp ginger purée
1 tbsp tomato purée
225ml coconut milk
250ml water
1 vegetable stock cube
50g baby spinach
1 tsp soy sauce

Preheat the oven to 220°c. Chop the sweet potatoes into 1cm chunks (no need to peel them). Pop the potatoes on a low-sided, wide baking tray. Use two baking trays if necessary as you want the potatoes nicely spread out. Drizzle them with oil, then season with salt and pepper. Toss to coat then spread out in a single layer. Once your oven is hot, roast the potatoes on the top shelf for 20-25 minutes until golden. Turn halfway through cooking.

Meanwhile, chop the tofu into 2cm cubes and pat dry with some kitchen paper. Heat a drizzle of oil in a large frying pan on medium-high heat. Once hot, add the tofu to the pan and fry for 6-8 minutes until golden all over, turning occasionally. Tip the tofu into a bowl and set aside. Keep the pan.

While the tofu cooks, halve, peel and thinly slice the shallot. Peel and grate the garlic (or use a garlic press). Thinly slice half the chilli and finely chop the rest. Zest and halve the lime.

Pop the pan back on a medium-high heat with a drizzle of oil. Once hot, add the shallot to the pan and fry for 3-4 minutes, until softened. Stir in the garlic, ginger purée, finely chopped chilli (add less if you don't like heat) and tomato purée, and cook for 1 minute. Pour in the coconut milk, water and vegetable stock cube. Bring to the boil and simmer until the sauce has reduced slightly, stirring occasionally. This should take 3-4 minutes. Stir in the spinach a handful at a time until it's wilted and everything is piping hot.

Remove from the heat, squeeze in some of the lime juice and add half the soy sauce. Taste and add more lime juice and soy sauce if you feel it needs it, then stir in the roasted sweet potato and tofu. Add a splash more water to the stew if it's a bit dry.

Serve in bowls with the sliced chilli (again, add less or leave this out if you don't like heat) and lime zest sprinkled on top. Enjoy!

Dr Victoria Bradley, Consultant in and Clinical Lead for Palliative Medicine at Sobell House

Queen of Puddings

This is my husband's great aunt's recipe for Queen of Puddings - she is an Oxon resident (in Ipsden just outside Wallingford) and a phenomenal cook. This is our favourite pudding, and a staple at any family celebration.

Preparation time: 50 minutes | Cooking time: 45-55 minutes | Serves: 6-8

570ml milk
10g butter
110g fresh white breadcrumbs
1 lemon, zested
50g caster sugar, plus 1 tsp for dusting
2 eggs
3 level tbsp raspberry jam

Preheat the oven to 180°c (160°c fan or Gas Mark 4) and generously butter a 1½ pint (845ml) oval pie dish.

First, pour the milk into a saucepan and bring to the boil. Remove from the heat and stir in the butter, breadcrumbs, lemon zest and 25g of the sugar, and then leave the mixture for 20 minutes to allow the breadcrumbs to swell.

Separate the eggs, putting the whites to one side. Beat the yolks and add them to the cooled breadcrumb mixture, then pour it all into the pie dish and spread out evenly. Bake in the centre of the oven for 30-35 minutes, or until set.

In the meantime, melt the jam in a small saucepan over a low heat and then, when the pudding is ready, remove it from the oven and spread the jam carefully and evenly all over the top.

Beat the egg whites until stiff, then whisk in the remaining 25g of the caster sugar and spoon this meringue mixture over the pudding.

Finally, sprinkle the teaspoon of caster sugar over the meringue and bake the pudding for a further 10-15 minutes until the topping is golden brown.

Consultant
Consultant

The Great Taste of the Mediterranean

Acropolis is devoted to bringing the best of Greece to your doorstep.

Acropolis was first opened in 2017 by two friends from Kurdistan, Iraq, who had lived in Greece for quite some time and understood the Greek culture and cuisine. The restaurant initially had a Kurdish chef closely connected with Greek culture.

The restaurant did very well in the first two years, and it was overwhelming for the owners at the time. Therefore, they decided to sell the restaurant and move on. In April 2019, two brothers, one with a degree in computer science and the other with a degree in biomedical sciences, decided to buy the restaurant and invest their money.

Their vision is to make Acropolis the number one destination for Greek food lovers in Oxfordshire. They started by ensuring the food was authentic, which involved making changes in the kitchen by employing a Greek chef from Chios Island in Greece, who has 30 years of experience.

Not long after taking over the restaurant, the COVID-19 pandemic hit the globe, and it was a great challenge to keep the restaurant afloat. The owners had to change their ways of working and adapt to keep up with the global pandemic.

Through dedication and smart decision-making, the restaurant came through the pandemic and is now one of the most popular restaurants in Oxford. They now have a wide range of customers from outside of Oxford who come to try the food on a regular basis.

Despite coming from a non-hospitality background, the two brothers' forward-thinking approach, coupled with a genuine love for food, has led to the success of the restaurant. Since their ownership began, the restaurant has been awarded the certificate of excellence by Trip Advisor for three years in a row.

ACROPOLIS GREEK TAVERNA
TAVERNA
01865
766 755
ACROPOLIS GREEK TAV

Gemista (Stuffed Vegetables)

Gemista or Yemista is a well-known dish in traditional Greek cuisine, consisting of peppers and tomatoes stuffed with rice, vegetables and herbs which are then baked in the oven.

Preparation time: 25 minutes | Cooking time: 1 hour 15 minutes | Serves: 2-3

2 aubergines
2 green or red peppers
6 Rosa tomatoes
200ml olive oil
2 tsp salt
1 tsp turmeric
2 medium red onions, finely chopped
1 courgette, cut into small pieces
2 cloves of garlic, finely chopped
50g black raisins
20g pine nuts
1 tsp white pepper
150g Carolina rice (long grain rice)
½ lemon
½ bunch of mint
½ bunch of parsley

First, prepare the aubergines, peppers and 2 of the tomatoes. Cut open all vegetables across the top or in half lengthways, then scoop out the insides to leave the shells. Place all the shells onto a tray and set the insides and cut offs aside for later.

To make the sauce, put the remaining tomatoes into a food processor with 100ml of the olive oil, 1 teaspoon of the salt and the turmeric. Blend until smooth.

In a frying pan, heat up the remaining olive oil and then add the chopped onions. Cook until brown, then add the inside of the aubergine and the diced courgette. On a low heat, add the garlic, raisins, pine nuts, remaining salt, and white pepper.

Rinse the rice with water and then squeeze the juice from the lemon half over the rice. Add it to the pan with half the tomato sauce, then pour in 200ml of hot water and cook for 5-6 minutes on a low heat. Finely chop the mint and parsley, then stir them into the mixture.

Spoon the filling into the aubergine, pepper and tomato shells. Cover them with the cut off pieces and then pour the rest of the tomato sauce over the stuffed vegetables. Cover the tray with foil.

Place the tray in the oven at 180°c and cook for 35 minutes. Take out the tray, take off the foil, and place back into the oven for another 40 minutes. The gemista is now ready to serve.

Down the Rabbit Hole

The Alice is an all-day British Brasserie in the heart of historic Oxford, serving comforting, seasonal British dishes with a contemporary twist.

Located within the city's cultural epicentre, The Randolph Hotel by Graduate Hotels takes inspiration from the University of Oxford's history, paying homage to its storied innovators and alumni. Just steps from iconic colleges, including St. Johns and Trinity, this historic landmark offers a retreat for locals and travellers alike.

There are six hospitality spaces within the Randolph Hotel including The Alice: The Alice Bar, The Morse Bar, The Snug, The Drawing Room and the Lancaster Room. The Alice offers a comforting à la carte menu every day of the week, plus a spectacular Sunday lunch: whole joints roasted the traditional way served with Yorkshire pudding, duck fat roast potatoes, a selection of seasonal vegetables and a big-hearted amount of Alice gravy.

Meanwhile in the Morse Bar, Drawing Room and Lancaster Room, guests can try the seasonal bar menu between 11am and 9.30pm. Drinks are available until midnight so pop in, pull up a chair and enjoy a broad range of bespoke and classic cocktails, wines and speciality beers. If a quintessentially British afternoon tea is more your thing, either The Alice, The Drawing Room or The Lancaster Room can satisfy your appetite (and sweet tooth!).

For those in-between times, visitors are welcome to relax in the intimate snug, a cosy nook between The Alice Brasserie and private dining rooms offering lighter bites and pre-or post-dinner drinks. The unique recipes for The Alice's cocktails and homemade cordials take inspiration from the hotel's surroundings and Oxford's history.

Private dining at The Alice Brasserie is perfect for birthdays, special parties and everyday get-togethers and you can also treat someone special with a gift voucher for afternoon tea, celebratory cocktails, Sunday lunch or a special dinner. Illustrations in the brasserie bring together its seasonal menu, the city of Oxford and ideas from the story Alice's Adventures in Wonderland. They take inspiration from the celebrated British cartoonist Osbert Lancaster, an erstwhile resident of The Randolph Hotel who paid for his keep in paintings.

Mushroom Risotto

This delicious dish is the perfect warming meal for cooler weather. Truffle paste adds a rich, earthy flavour that accentuates the wild mushrooms.

Preparation time: 30 minutes | Cooking time: 20 minutes | Serves: 4

800ml mushroom stock
25g butter
30g onion or shallot, finely chopped
175g carnaroli rice
100ml white wine
400g wild mushrooms
30g truffle paste
80g cold butter, diced
100g parmesan or Grana Padano, grated
Salt and pepper

Heat the mushroom stock in a pan and keep at a near simmer. Heat the butter in a separate heavy-bottomed pan over a medium heat and add the onion. Cook for about 5 minutes until soft and tender but with no colour. Turn up the heat, add the rice and stir using a wooden spatula until the grains are well coated in butter and onions, and heated through, again with no colour. It is important to get the grains up to a hot temperature before adding the wine.

Turn the heat up to high, add the wine (it should sizzle) and reduce until almost all of the wine has evaporated. Once it has reduced, add a ladle of the hot mushroom stock while stirring constantly. The rice should always be coated with stock, but not swamped or drowning in liquid.

Once the stock has been absorbed, add the next ladle of stock, stirring to keep the rice moving. The risotto should be steadily cooking and bubbling. From start to finish this process should take about 17-18 minutes. The rice is ready when it is plump and tender, but the centre of the grain still has a slight firmness to the bite. When you've achieved this, remove the pan from the heat and leave the risotto to cool for a minute.

Meanwhile, sauté the wild mushrooms in a separate pan with a little butter or oil until they have a nice colour but have not softened too much. Stir the mushrooms into the risotto along with the truffle paste, then add the diced cold butter and beat into the risotto. This helps to create a creamy emulsion. Finally, add the grated parmesan, beating it into the risotto, then taste and adjust the seasoning if necessary. Spoon the risotto into warmed bowls and serve immediately.

Business is Bhooming!

Bringing the food of southern India to southern England, Bhoomi Kitchen is a place of authenticity and innovation, with branches in Cheltenham and Oxford.

Bhoomi Kitchen's story begins over 6,000 miles away, in the small South Indian village of Kaliyar, Kerala. It was in this village that farmer Appacha first discovered his love for food, cooking, and hospitality. Tales of his vibrant dishes and hospitable service returned to the English farm owner, who soon called upon Appacha to live and work in his farm house in Burford. Appacha accepted and brought with him his authentic southern Indian dishes, much to the approval and delight of the owner's friends, family, and neighbours. With recognisable and undeniable talent, Appacha finally settled in Cheltenham, where he worked for years as a private chef.

Now, almost 50 years later, Appacha is the inspiration to his grandson Michael, who has reignited the tastes and authenticity of Appacha's southern Indian dishes, which he now serves to you in the form of Bhoomi Kitchen. After working on the format, developing menus and securing a venue, he opened Bhoomi Kitchen in Cheltenham, with an Oxford branch following in 2020. The concept quickly caught on thanks to the casual but high end vibe, upbeat atmosphere and vibrant food.

The relaxed restaurants allow diners to mix and match between sections of the menu. There are classic dishes such as traditional Keralan curries, thali for speedy but delicious pre-theatre meals, small plates for sharing and Indian barbecue, all freshly prepared by specialist chefs. It was important for these parts of southern Indian culture to be expressed with such flexible food, alongside a fun selection of Indian-inspired cocktails and plenty of beer or lassi to complement the charcoal-grilled meats and vegetarian or vegan dishes. Bhoomi Kitchen also serves an unusual pork tenderloin curry alongside the beef and lamb specials, showcasing a wide range of southern Indian cuisine which is often less represented here in the UK.

Despite coming from a background in retail, Michael's forward-thinking approach coupled with a genuine love of food, including his own culinary heritage, has led to great success as a restaurateur. Having made a life-changing move into something he'd always wanted to do, he found a balance between family and business that allows Bhoomi Kitchen to flourish. Since then, it has been listed in the Michelin Guide and Harden's Guide, won the Taste of Gloucestershire Award in 2016 and was named Best Restaurant in the South West by the Asian Curry Awards.

INDIAN BBQ &
SOUTH INDIAN PLATES
BHOOMI KITCHEN

Aloo Bonda

An easy to make and delicious snack from the street stalls of Kerala. All the ingredients can easily be found in your local Asian supermarket.

Preparation time: 15 minutes | Cooking time: 30 minutes | Serves: 10-12

For the potato mixture

5 potatoes
4 tbsp oil, for frying
1 tsp mustard seeds
1 tsp white lentils (urid dal)
A few curry leaves
A small piece of ginger, finely chopped
3 onions, finely chopped
½ tsp ground turmeric
Fresh coriander, chopped
Salt, to taste

For the batter

375g chickpea flour
2 tbsp rice flour
½ tsp asafoetida (hing)
½ tsp ground turmeric

For the potato mixture

First, boil the potatoes until tender and then drain. While the potatoes steam dry, heat the oil in a frying pan and add the mustard seeds, cooking them until they start to crack.

Next, add the white lentils, curry leaves and ginger to the frying pan and sauté for 3 minutes. Add the onions and sauté for a further 5 minutes before mixing in the boiled potatoes and turmeric. Mix well and mash before adding the fresh coriander and salt to taste.

For the batter

Put all the ingredients in a bowl and mix well with just enough water to make a smooth, creamy consistency. Form the potato mixture into balls and dip each one into the batter, ensuring they're completely covered. Deep fry them over a medium heat until golden brown and serve hot.

Florence Pugh, Actress

Tzatziki

My favourite dip on Earth is from Greek cuisine. I'm sure many people who have grown up on the dip will have better and more skilled versions of it, but this is my quick and easy to please dinner dip that will leave your hosts wanting more, with intense garlicky breath... Trust me, it's worth it!

Preparation time: 10 minutes | Serves: 2-4

½ a cucumber
2 cloves of garlic (fresh garlic will get stronger over time, so if you prefer less just use 1 clove!)
450g Greek yoghurt (I use Fage Total 5%)
Heavy handful of salt
Pinch of black pepper
Drizzle of olive oil
Oregano, to garnish

First, grate the cucumber on the large side of a box grater (the one you would use for cheddar). Once done, clasp it in your hands and squeeze out the liquid. This will help the consistency of the finished dip. Throw that green handful into a large bowl.

Next, either finely dice or finely grate the two cloves of garlic. Don't waste the butts! Chop them up and add them to the bowl.

Now add the yoghurt, salt and pepper. Stir. Taste it, then add more of any seasoning to your liking.

Drizzle the olive oil into the mixture and stir again to create a smooth texture.

I plate the tzatziki on my most favourite platter, drizzle it again with olive oil for a tasty decoration, then sprinkle some oregano (if you have some – it's not detrimental to the dish if not) over the top.

Serve with bread, pita, crackers, crudités, pizza crusts, gyros, pork, kebabs... anything! It's always partnered best with anything you fancy. Even if you have none of the above, I just spoon it out with cutlery or a finger! Enjoy.

Florence is a well-known actress and was born in Oxford. In the 2020 lockdowns during the Covid-19 pandemic, Florence used her social media platform to inspire others to spend their time cooking, and we are so grateful that she is supporting Sobell House through our own cookbook.

HEARD
HOTEL

Creating Culinary Magic

Café Coco, Kazbar and Café Tarifa share a location and an owner, but each has an individual style that Oxford has enjoyed since the first opening in 1992.

Café Coco opened on Cowley Road in Oxford over 30 years ago and has been winning awards and loyal support ever since. Coco prides itself on the friendly service, buzzing atmosphere, great cocktails and lip smacking food, including healthy breakfast options and gluten-free dishes. It's a popular spot for brunch and lunch with a tempting menu of indulgent burgers and steaks, pizzas featuring international toppings and flavour-packed salads. Drawing on international culinary influences, the café offers a balance of naughty but nice and 'superfood' dishes to suit all palates.

Owner and founder Clinton Pugh, an experienced restaurateur who has run various venues around Oxford, explains how sustainability has also become even more important to his food: "after watching Seaspiracy I felt that I had to make some changes to my menu, so we now use line-caught smoked haddock in the kedgeree and have replaced salmon with trout from North Devon which is raised in the natural environment of freshwater springs rather than farmed. It's not always easy to source sustainable alternatives but we try our best."

Clinton has also owned and run Kazbar for over 20 years, which is situated next door to Café Coco. Known for friendly smiles, beautifully handmade food, and delicious cocktails, the Oxford tapas bar also shares an outdoor seating area with its sister business. Whatever the time of year, Kazbar is the perfect place to sit back and soak up the atmosphere in a strongly design-led space that draws on Moorish influences from Spanish architecture.

It's thanks to the "fantastic team" who work across all three venues that Clinton continues to run his restaurants with such success. This hard-working group of employees has included all four of his children at various times – Arabella, Sebastian, Florence and Rafaella – making it very much a family business. "Hospitality is a great industry to meet people: actors, musicians, designers," says Clinton. The Oxford-based band Supergrass are longstanding customers of Café Coco, in fact, even taking one of their album names from a sign on the building's exterior wall saying 'I should Coco'! Clinton himself is also a designer by trade and his children have all pursued acting careers, so creativity runs in the family and is evident at the three unique café bars on Oxford's thriving Cowley Road.

CøCø
RESTAURANT · CAFE · BAR
RESTAURANT · CAFE · BAR
TAKE AWAY PIZZA
RESTAURANT
CAFÉ
CøCø
ESTABLISHED 1992
CAFE · BAR
RESTAURANT
CAFÉ
CøCø
CAFE · BAR
GRAND-HOTEL
DJOKJA
Java
TOBY SEBASTIAN
HAPPY HOURS

Vegan Burger

When I decided to put on a vegan burger at Café Coco it didn't take me long to realise that I needed to create a healthy recipe myself. It's not trying to be meat but a tasty, healthy alternative.

Preparation time: 20 minutes | Cooking time: 8 minutes | Serves: 4-6

400g cooked black beans (or rinsed and drained tinned black beans)
150g grated carrot
130g red onion, finely diced
80g oats
15g garlic, finely diced
7.5g sea salt
5g ground cumin
5g ground coriander
5g cracked black pepper
3g chilli powder or 20g fresh red chilli, finely diced
60g flax seeds
Polenta, to coat
Rapeseed oil, to cook
Bread rolls or burger buns
Hummus or tzatziki (optional)

To make the burgers

Blend the cooked black beans with the carrot, onion, oats, garlic, salt, and spices in a food processor for approximately 6 minutes at medium speed. Add the flax seeds and blend at a lower speed for a further 3 minutes.

Cover the base of a wide, shallow bowl with polenta. Now make the patties; we use a terracotta tapas dish to standardise the portions. Lay some cling film over the dish and fill it with the black bean mixture. Push into the dish until flat, then turn out and place the burger patty into the bowl of polenta and coat the outer surface. Repeat to use up all the black bean mixture.

To cook the burgers

Shallow fry the burger patties on both sides until crisp. We use rapeseed oil in the restaurant but you could also use pomace oil or olive oil, although be careful not to over heat the olive oil.

To assemble the burgers

At Café Coco we toast our buns and then dress them with lettuce, slices of tomato and picked dill. Add the black bean patties and then top with hummus or tzatziki if you like; both work wonderfully and can be easily whipped up at home or shop-bought. I personally like to also add tomato ketchup and mayonnaise. YUMMY!

Welcomed with Open Arms

Set in a beautiful Oxfordshire village, The Eyston Arms is a haven for loyal customers as well as those new to its charms, where good pub food is always the order of the day.

The Eyston Arms in East Hendred is a proper English pub with great food at its heart. The day-to-day running is handled by Daisy Barton, one of three partners who established the business with George Dailey and Edward Eyston over twenty years ago. Chef Maria Jaremchuk has headed the kitchen for over 18 years, and Lidia Dhorne is the restaurant manager who Daisy describes as "wonderfully capable and brilliant with customers". The longstanding team is testament to the great atmosphere at The Eyston Arms which has also kept customers coming back over the years, along with delicious food and drink of course.

The menu is a lovely mix of traditional pub favourites for those who love potted shrimps, a burger or fish and chips on a Friday, but also features something a bit different to tickle the taste buds, from tapas to duck panang curry, wild seabass and classic pastry puddings. The emphasis is on variety rather than endless options and dishes change all the time based on seasonal produce, some of which comes with the customers from their nearby allotments! The pub also uses local suppliers where possible including an award-winning butcher, Vicar's Game, and has a fish delivery six days a week from Kingfisher in Brixham to ensure the fish is of the highest and freshest quality.

Being a freehouse means the drinks offering can get just as interesting, though you'll nearly always find an old favourite on tap in the form of Wadworth 6X alongside other local beers and ciders. The Eyston Arms also boasts a selection of gins and whiskies, a wine list, and most importantly a friendly, approachable bar with a great atmosphere to enjoy it all in. Being housed in a very old building helps to set the scene: flagstone floors, an open fire, wooden beams and a succession of little rooms (including private dining for up to 12 or 20 in the bar) create a cosy setting for any occasion. During the pandemic they also invested in the outdoor area with a permanent canopy over the terrace for all-weather drinking and dining.

"The thing that really matters to us is serving really good food in a pub," explains Daisy, "so we welcome dogs, families, young and old...the pub sees a huge number of returning customers who we love. They kept us alive during the lockdowns by coming in for takeaways, and in a world where most of us work on computers all day, it's wonderful to be surrounded by people here – it makes for a magical atmosphere."

The Eyston Arms
THE EYSTON ARMS
THE EYSTON ARMS

Rhubarb, Pistachio and Orange Tart

We love rhubarb at The Eyston Arms! This is Maria's very easy, if slightly time-consuming recipe, which uses all our favourite ingredients and has gone down exceptionally well with our customers.

Preparation time: 3 hours | Cooking time: 30-45 minutes | Serves: 12-14

For the sweet shortcrust pastry
400g plain flour
50g caster sugar
200g cold diced unsalted butter
1 egg, cold water if needed

For the filling
225g unsalted butter
225g sieved caster sugar
1 large orange, zested and juiced
55g plain flour & 1 tsp baking powder
3 eggs, plus an extra yolk
250g ground almonds
55g ground or blitzed pistachios
400g rhubarb

For the pistachio sugar
30g blitzed pistachios
30g caster sugar

For the glaze
10 tbsp water & 6 tbsp caster sugar
½ orange, juiced

For the rhubarb purée
Rhubarb trim
4 tbsp sugar
10 tbsp water
½ tsp vanilla paste
Squeeze of orange juice

Line a 30 by 4cm loose-bottomed pastry tin with greaseproof paper.

For the pastry

Sift the flour into a large bowl, stir in the sugar and then rub in the diced butter. Add the egg to bind the mixture, along with a little cold water if needed.

Roll out the pastry to fit the tin and trim the edges. It will be crumbly but don't worry, just patch up any holes with the trim. Chill for a minimum of 2 hours.

For the filling

Cream the butter and sugar together. Add the orange zest and juice, sift the flour and baking powder into the mix and then add the eggs, yolk, ground almonds and pistachios. Fold together until mixed.

Top and tail the rhubarb and keep the trim to one side for later. Cut the stalks into 1 inch chunks and toss them in some sugar. Put the filling into the chilled pastry case and scatter the rhubarb chunks on top.

Bake the tart on the bottom shelf of a fan assisted oven at 190°c for 12 minutes. Reduce the temperature to 175°c for a further 12 minutes, then reduce again to 155°c and continue to cook until set. Meanwhile, make the pistachio sugar by blitzing the pistachios and sugar together. Make the glaze by combining all the ingredients in a pan and boiling until a light syrup forms.

Glaze the top of the tart while warm and sprinkle with the pistachio sugar. If you like, use the remaining rhubarb trim to make a purée by blitzing it with the sugar, water and vanilla paste. Add a squeeze of orange juice and adjust the sweetness to taste.

We like to serve this with some sweetened mascarpone and fresh basil.

Good Food and Green Thumbs

Opened in 2003 to provide quality vegan and vegetarian food that would appeal to all diners in a pub setting, The Gardeners Arms is a quirky Oxford treasure that's not to be missed.

The story of The Gardeners Arms can be traced back all the way to 1789, which is the first record of the pub on Oxford's Plantation Road. However, the business as it is today started 19 years ago when Andy Skinner, the head chef, saw a gap in the market and decided to take an approach that was fairly radical back then: to have a completely vegetarian and vegan kitchen. Tired of having nowhere to take his vegan family, Andy set out to create a place he'd want to take them for a meal out, and so The Gardeners Arms was reborn.

It still holds the title of Oxford's oldest serving 100% vegetarian and vegan kitchen, in a pub that regularly makes The Good Beer Guide and has the only turfed beer garden in Jericho. The alleyway to this lovely hidden area is something of an indoor garden itself, with many plants growing from baskets and pots. Rather appropriately, the pub's name comes from the many allotments that existed in the area 200 years ago. There also happens to be a second Gardeners Arms less than five minutes away, which causes some confusion for those who aren't local!

The Gardeners Arms has a homey feel – customers often describe it like a cosy front room – and is a pub for all weathers, all year round. The landlord's own vinyl collection adorns the walls, generating interest especially amongst customers of a certain age who recognise musical gems from the past. It serves all the traditional pub food you would expect to find, just 100% vegetarian and vegan. There are several standouts on the menu including the mushroom pie, Mexican chilli and kebab bowls, but the customer favourite is the Quarter Pound Burger.

"We've tried changing the menu but there was public outcry," says Andy. "We do, however, have specials so we can try out new dishes." With nearly two decades of success, happy customers and a happy family to boot, The Gardeners Arms is a stand out spot for meat-free meals that everyone will get stuck into.

THE GARDENERS ARMS
FREE HOUSE
THE GARDENERS ARMS
FREE HOUSE

Vegan Chicken Caesar Style Salad

Chicken Caesar salad is a great option for lunch or a light dinner, and this version is easy to throw together at home in no time. You can use whichever vegan chicken substitute you prefer.

Preparation time: 20 minutes | Cooking time: 5 minutes | Serves: 4

2 thick slices of white bread
Dried oregano
Salt and pepper
Extra virgin olive oil
4 heaped tbsp good quality vegan mayo (Hellman's or Heinz is ideal)
4 tsp lemon juice (freshly squeezed or from a bottle)
4 tsp yellow burger mustard
Vegan chicken pieces, cooked to instructions on packet
1 iceberg or 2 cos (Romaine) lettuce, hearts removed and sliced into 1-inch strips (and washed!)
½ cucumber, deseeded and chopped into 2cm cubes
Nutritional yeast flakes
A mild grated vegan mozzarella cheese
2 tbsp chopped fresh flat leaf parsley

To make the croutons, preheat the oven to 220°c or Gas Mark 7. Remove the crusts from the bread and slice into cubes. Place them on a baking tray, lightly season with the oregano, salt and pepper, then drizzle with olive oil.

Place the tray in the oven for a few minutes, occasionally taking it out and turning the bread, until the croutons have started to brown (keep a watchful eye as you don't want them to burn) and then set aside to cool.

To make the dressing, combine the vegan mayo, lemon juice and mustard in a small bowl and mix thoroughly.

To assemble the salad, put the warm vegan chicken pieces in a bowl with the croutons and toss together gently.

Put a quarter of the lettuce into each serving bowl and scatter the chopped cucumber over the top. Evenly divide the crouton and chicken mix between the bowls, on top of the beds of lettuce.

Use a tablespoon to drizzle the salad with your dressing, then top with a pinch of nutritional yeast and a light sprinkle of the grated vegan cheese. Finish with the chopped parsley.

Huw Edwards, BBC Journalist, Presenter and Newsreader

Burrata with Broad Bean and Almond Pesto

This recipe is by my son Sammy who's an excellent cook. I am proud to support all the staff of Sobell House for the essential care they offer people in the most challenging circumstances.

Preparation time: 15-20 minutes | Cooking time: 5 minutes |Serves: 4

4 burrata
300g podded peas
300g fresh broad beans
Fresh mint, roughly chopped
Extra virgin olive oil
Sourdough, to serve

For the pesto
320g fresh broad beans
50g parmesan
50g blanched whole almonds (set some aside for plating)
20g picked basil leaves
10g picked mint leaves
½ lemon, zested
½ clove of garlic
130ml extra virgin olive oil
Salt and pepper

For the pesto, start by podding the broad beans. Blanch them for 90 seconds in boiling salted water, then refresh in iced water before peeling off the skins. Blitz the beans with all the other pesto ingredients except for the oil in a food processor. Once blended to a rough paste, add the oil in a slow stream. Season with salt and pepper to taste. Set aside.

Bring a pan of salted water to the boil. Cook the peas until tender. Refresh them in iced water, then set aside. Blanch the broad beans in the same water for 1 minute, then refresh them in iced water. Once cooled, remove their skins and place in a bowl with the peas. Dress the peas and broad beans with some roughly chopped mint, olive oil, salt and pepper to taste.

When ready to serve, drain the burrata on kitchen paper and grate some lemon zest over them. Place a generous spoon of the pesto on the plate. Top this with the dressed peas and broad beans, followed by the burrata. Sprinkle over the reserved almonds, and drizzle with olive oil. Serve with a thick slice of toasted sourdough.

We were delighted that Huw spoke at one of our virtual business lunches during lockdown and since then has become a good friend to Sobell House.

Time to Treat Yourself

Jolly Good Brownies is what the name suggests and more: irresistible squidgy chocolate indulgence, made to order and delivered to your door!

Oli Barton had been making brownies "forever" for friends, family and clients when a next-door neighbour suggested she turn the treats into a new business venture. Having been a caterer for many years, and a trained chef, Oli felt that going back to all the evenings and weekends of work with her three children now in the picture just wasn't appealing.

So instead, she set up Jolly Good Brownies from home in 2018 and began a mail-order service that delivers her brownies right across the UK. Using her original recipe as the starting point, Oli developed more flavours and varieties to offer something for everyone. You can now choose from salted caramel, chocolate orange, Toblerone, gluten-free and low-sugar brownies for children, as well as raw vegan fruit and nut bars, which you can find the recipe for in the first Sobell House cook book! Jolly Good Brownies make great presents as they come gift wrapped and can be sent anywhere in the country. The ordering process is all online, and there are gift boxes for various special occasions from birthdays to new babies (aimed at the sleep-deprived parents, of course!) although you can always treat yourself too.

The interest of local people, word of mouth, and then social media played a big part in growing sales for the fledgling company, alongside Oli's enterprising partnerships with other local independents. Her brownie boxes can include add-ons such as Neal's Yard products, hand creams from Oxford Soap Company and local maker Cucumber Wood's scented candles to make gifting more personalised. Oli also has an important connection to Sobell House, as both her father and mother-in-law were cared for by the amazing team at Sobell House towards the end of their lives.

All Oli's brownies are freshly made to order, using free-range eggs and high quality ingredients to make them jolly good. The company name was suggested by a friend as 'Bloody Good Brownies' but when their son (then five years old) overheard wrongly while Oli and her husband were discussing it, he decided that Jolly Good Brownies was the perfect fit! The company has certainly lived up to its name, having been shortlisted for the 2020 South Vale Business Awards as a New Startup. Oli is hoping to expand in the near future, moving to a commercial premises and growing her current team of one so Jolly Good Brownies can reach more people.

Jolly Good Brownies
Jolly Good Brownies
Jolly Good Brownies
Jolly Good Brownies
Jolly Good Brownies

Baileys Coffee and Chocolate Cake

Whilst I can't share my top secret brownie recipe with you, this deliciously indulgent cake is one of my absolute favourite recipes: so easy to make and the perfect show stopper to pull out at a party. Including Baileys is the perfect excuse not to share with the children too!

Preparation time: 30 minutes | Cooking time: 50 minutes to 1 hour | Serves: 12

For the cake
170g self-raising flour
60g cocoa powder
1 tsp bicarbonate of soda
275g caster sugar
2 medium eggs, beaten
85ml vegetable oil
180ml milk
1 tsp vanilla extract
4 tsp instant coffee
180ml boiling water

For the icing
250g salted butter, at room temperature
500g icing sugar
3 tbsp Baileys Irish Cream

For the decoration
100g white chocolate
10 strawberries
50g dark chocolate

For the cake

Preheat the oven to 180°c. Grease and line an 8 inch cake tin with baking parchment.

Sift the flour, cocoa powder and bicarbonate of soda into a bowl, then add the caster sugar.

Beat in the eggs and vegetable oil until smooth. Gradually add the milk and vanilla extract to the bowl. Dissolve the instant coffee in the boiling water and gradually add this to the mixture until it is all incorporated. Pour the batter into the cake tin and bake on the middle shelf of the preheated oven for 50 minutes to 1 hour. The cake is ready when a skewer inserted into the middle of the cake comes out clean. Allow the cake to cool fully in the tin.

For the icing

Whisk the butter until soft using a hand whisk or electric mixer. Gradually add the icing sugar and continue to whisk until light and fluffy, then gradually add the Baileys until incorporated.

Remove the cooled cake from the tin and slice in half horizontally. Spread a generous layer of icing over the bottom layer and then sandwich with the top layer. Spread the remaining icing over the top and sides of the cake.

For the decoration

Melt the white chocolate in a bowl set over a saucepan of simmering water. Dip the strawberries in the white chocolate until half covered and leave to cool and set on a sheet of baking parchment. Melt the dark chocolate in a bowl set over a saucepan of simmering water and drizzle it over the strawberries. Once set, arrange the chocolate-covered strawberries in the centre of the cake.
If you're feeling extra adventurous, you can make shards of white chocolate by spreading a thin layer of melted white chocolate onto baking parchment, sprinkling with freeze-dried strawberries (available from most supermarkets), then leaving to set before cutting into triangles.

Old Stories are the Best

Take a walk into the heart of Jericho and you'll find a traditional pub specialising in real ales and bistro-style food, home to local punters and a community for the people of Oxford.

The Old Bookbinders Ale House is not your standard gastropub, priding itself on being an authentic and traditional watering hole serving high quality food. Josh and his father Michel have run the family-owned pub since 2011, when the former caterers decided they couldn't pass up the opportunity to become publicans in such a special setting. The friendly atmosphere they have encouraged reflects the community feel of the area; Jericho is home to many small independent businesses where "everybody knows everybody" and is located just 10 minutes' walk from the city centre.

The Old Bookbinders is a pub rich in history and is truly one of a kind, housed in a 150-year-old building that retains its original features to create a traditional feel and aesthetic. Its unusual name is unique to the pub and originates from the workers of Oxford University Press who were commemorated by its establishment in 1869. The family-oriented atmosphere has resulted in many returning customers over the years, for whom the pub has become their second home.

Serving a range of bistro-style French food, the menu is prepared by Michel Sadones, a professional chef and restaurateur who hails from Normandy, France, and has run many establishments throughout the UK since 1980. The Old Bookbinders offers a range of lunch and dinner dishes but is known for the infamous crepes, a speciality loved by all. The kitchen team source their produce from local suppliers, including organic and free-range British meat. With seasonal changes to the menu, signature dishes include Moules Marinière with garlic bread on the Friday specials, alongside escargot, steak-frites, and many more. The pub also specialises in real ale and has been listed in the Good Beer Guide.

Josh and his family have always focused on the importance of great service too, ensuring their staff enjoy a good working environment which in turn creates a good atmosphere for customers. If you're looking for a historical pub with quality food and a great community, The Old Bookbinders should be top of your list for your next visit to Oxford!

BEER
CHÂTEAU
BORDEAUX
2019
BOOKBINDERS
OLD BOOKBINDERS

Le Cassoulet Méditerranéen

This cassoulet has been created to give you all the rustic flavours of your typical French dish but make it wholeheartedly vegan! We love the addition of smoked tofu to give it a bit of variation in texture and an added depth of flavour.

Preparation time: 30 minutes (or 5 hours if using dried beans) | Cooking time: 1 hour 30 minutes | Serves: 6

150g dried red kidney beans
150g dried cannellini beans
(if short on time, use 1 tin of mixed beans and 1 tin of cannellini beans instead)
800g peeled tomatoes
1 tbsp caster sugar
1 tsp cayenne pepper
1 tsp ground cumin
1 tsp chilli flakes
1 small aubergine
1 courgette
1 of each colour bell pepper
1 red onion
Olive oil
Sea salt and black pepper, to taste
12 vegan sausages (we love Taste & Glory sausages!)
150g smoked tofu
1 bag of baby spinach

Soak your beans for at least 5 hours prior to starting the recipe. Overnight works best! Skip this step if using tinned beans.

To make the sauce, put the peeled tomatoes into a large saucepan on a low-medium heat. Add the sugar, cayenne, cumin, and chilli flakes. Stir to mix in the spices and leave on a low heat for 40 minutes to reduce slightly.

While the sauce is cooking, start on the Mediterranean veg. Heat a baking tray in an oven set to 200°c. Dice the vegetables into 2cm pieces, keeping them all a similar size to aid even cooking times.

When your oven is hot, add the vegetables to the preheated baking tray with a generous drizzle of olive oil, sea salt and black pepper.

Roast for 15 minutes, then take the tray out and mix the vegetables. Drizzle with a little more oil and some more salt. Return for the oven for another 15 minutes until the vegetables are starting to char in a few places.

Using another baking tray, pop your sausages in the oven for 15-20 minutes, or as per the packet instructions. When cooked, chop into bite-sized pieces.

Once your tomatoes have reduced in the saucepan, blend them into a smooth sauce.

To serve

Combine the beans, roasted vegetables, sausages, and tomato sauce in the saucepan. Cook on the hob for another 15 minutes on a medium heat. Cube the smoked tofu and stir it into this mixture. Cover the bottom of each serving dish with a layer of baby spinach, spoon the cassoulet on top and then serve with a side of crusty bread.

The Finest Catering for Every Eventuality

The Oxford Fine Dining team are a collection of seasoned, passionate experts who bring unrivalled knowledge and skill to every event. They strive for consistent excellence in all they do and support this with a friendly, hands-on approach.

Oxford Fine Dining has built up many strong working relationships over the years, not least with Sobell House for which it fundraises regularly alongside catering for some of the city's most prestigious venues and events. Making and maintaining good relationships is at the heart of the Oxford Fine Dining ethos, and it's this commitment to clients and local suppliers that makes the catering company a preferred choice throughout Oxfordshire and the Cotswolds. Their chefs use innovation and creativity to ensure deliciously different menus at each special occasion and are extremely proud of the trusted reputation they have gained over the past 15 years.

Sue Randall co-owns Oxford Fine Dining with her business partner Della Hutton; they started the company in 2007 with firm roots in hospitality and a desire for excellence. They are supported by the senior management team: Melissa Bennett – Wedding and Events Director, Norma Bennett – Finance Director, and Willis Smith – Head Chef. Sue describes the team as close-knit and Oxford Fine Dining is very much a family business.

Customers might be attending a conference where the team have laid on a banquet for 1000 people or enjoying canapés at a reception; the experienced caterers can provide "pretty much anything" including open fire cooking, which they introduced for the Shakespeare's Rose Theatre pop-up at Blenheim in summer 2019. Other highlights include catering for HRH The Prince of Wales, the Dalai Lama, The Rolling Stones and Bono.

The chefs produce a menu for every season, making the best of local produce while allowing enough flexibility to ensure the food and drink is customised for each event. Each year, the caterers also participate in one of the city's most famous sporting events, the Oxford and Cambridge Boat Race, where they provide canapés and bowl food for VIP spectators in London.

Oxford Fine Dining also hosts an annual menu showcase to support Sobell House, as a member of the charity's Business Club. Each attendee donates £10 for the chance to win a catered dining experience at home, often raising over £1000 in total. "We enjoy this event as it gives us a chance to catch up and thank our customers and suppliers, while showcasing what we do at our best," says Sue, "but we also want to give back to the community. When Sobell House got in touch, the more we spoke to friends and family the more we realised how many personal ties connected us to the hospice, so it just felt right."

OXFORD fine DINING
OXFORD fine DINING
THE finest CATERING
FOR EVERY EVENTUALITY
MENUS
NEGROAMARO
CHARDONNAY
PROSECCO
BORGA

Lentil Dhal with Kachumber Salad

I have added spices to our usual lentil dhal to create a more fragrant and luscious version. When I experienced some time in India, I discovered that their base of spices was a lot more varied which inspired me to extend the flavour profile of this dish.

Preparation time: 20 minutes | Cooking time: 40 minutes | Serves: 2

For the lentil dhal
2 white onions, finely diced
3 cloves of garlic, finely sliced
1-2 red chillies (depending on how spicy you like it)
Small knob of ginger, finely chopped
2 tsp each fenugreek powder, ground coriander & curry powder
1 tsp ground turmeric
1 tsp smoked paprika
1 tsp garam each masala & ground cumin
1 cinnamon stick
4 plum tomatoes, roughly diced
1 x 400g tin of chopped tomatoes
200g coconut milk
200g red lentils, soaked in water overnight
1 cauliflower, cut into 2-3cm florets

For the kachumber salad
¼ large cucumber
¼ red onion & ½ red chilli
1 spring onion & 3 sprigs of mint
25g fresh coriander
60g pomegranate seeds
½ tsp black onion seeds
1 tsp white wine vinegar
1 tsp olive oil

For the lentil dhal

In a pan, heat a good glug of oil and start to slowly add some colour to the onion and garlic. Once some colour is there, add the finely chopped chilli and ginger. Cook for another 2-3 minutes.

Stir in all the spices and add a bit more oil so they can cook with the onions. Add the diced plum tomatoes and once the liquid has started to come out, add the tinned chopped tomatoes and coconut milk.

Add the lentils and slowly cook down until they are soft and tender. If the dhal seems to be getting a bit dry, add a splash of water until it's the right consistency for you.

Meanwhile, roast the cauliflower florets in a hot oven until just tender, then stir them through the dhal when both are cooked.

For the kachumber salad

Peel the cucumber and dice into medium cubes. Finely chop the red onion and red chilli, removing the seeds, then thinly slice the spring onion. Take the leaves of the mint sprigs and finely chop them along with the coriander.

Combine all the prepared ingredients in a bowl with the pomegranate seeds, black onion seeds, white wine vinegar and olive oil until everything is well mixed.

Serve the kachumber salad alongside your lentil dahl.

Matt Allwright, Television Presenter and Journalist

Mean and Moody Chilli Jam

This is what happened when I didn't have the right ingredients to make chilli jam as per a recipe. I had to substitute the delicious soft brown sugar instead of caster sugar. I also over-egged the scotch bonnets, so it ended up much stronger than intended. The result was a New Orleans style, dark, molasses-like chilli jam with a kick like an actual mule, which I loved. If you want it tamer, just halve the number of scotch bonnets or use a bit less!

Preparation time: 5 minutes | Cooking time: 1 hour | Makes 4 jam jars

10 scotch bonnet or habanero peppers, chopped
6 red peppers, deseeded and chopped
6 cloves of garlic, peeled
A chunk of root ginger, peeled and chopped
400g tinned tomatoes
750g soft dark brown sugar
250ml cider vinegar

Whizz the chillies, peppers, garlic and ginger up in a blender. The fumes should make your eyes water a bit. Stick the whole lot in a pan with a thick bottom, and mix it up with the tomatoes, sugar and vinegar.

Bring to the boil, then let it sit and simmer, skimming the stuff off the surface, and occasionally stirring to prevent burning on the bottom until the whole lot looks like jam and is burping and farting. It should take about an hour.

Funnel the jam into sterilised jars and keep for three months tops, in the fridge once opened. Better still, double up the quantities and give away to your friends. If nothing else, you'll soon find out who your friends are.

Matt has been friends with our Sobell House Music Therapist, Tom Crook, since they were teenagers. "Tom is incredible," says Matt. "He has committed his life to music and now uses it in the most beautiful way. I'm glad to be able to support him and all the work that Sobell does."

Sunday Roasts Have a New Look

Parsonage Grill is famous for its intimate, bohemian, clubby atmosphere, where head chef Allan McLaughlin and his team take pride in creating classic British dishes with a modern, light touch.

Brought to life in 1989 by experienced restaurateur and hotelier Jeremy Mogford, Parsonage Grill is a Cotswold-esque bolthole located within the 5-star 17th century Old Parsonage Hotel, rooted in central Oxford on Banbury Road. The Old Parsonage building has stood on its present site since 1660, when Edward Selwood, the prosperous chef of nearby St John's College, completed the original and principal part of the house, which he had begun twenty years earlier. The land on which Selwood built his house belonged to University College, one of Oxford's oldest seats of learning which had bought the land as an endowment for their early scholars. The college has remained the ground landlord for over six centuries.

Jeremy Mogford and his architect Roger Stretton set about a refurbishment scheme to restore the character of the original building. They sought to bring the atmosphere of the old house into the remaining more recent areas by using traditional materials, details and furnishings with the watchful approval of the preservation and heritage authorities. From a 17th century guesthouse to the present elegant hotel, the Old Parsonage continues to be a haven of good hospitality and has become a well-loved feature of Oxford.

Parsonage Grill and the private dining space, the 'Pike Room', feature walls adorned with a carefully curated collection of eclectic oil paintings, original stone fireplaces, leaded light windows and a Bloomsbury club ambience throughout, accompanied by a charming walled terrace set in view of a 400-year-old wisteria.

Carrying down the element of tradition from the glory days of Selwood's guesthouse to the ever-changing seasonal menus, and with a state-of-the-art kitchen, head chef Allan McLaughlin and his team take pride in using the best local produce to create classic, simple yet innovative British dishes. Open every day of the year, enjoy breakfast, lunch, dinner and famous afternoon teas in the company of Oxford's academic and literary luminaries, and where Oscar Wilde once sought refuge.

A renowned Oxford institution, the Parsonage Grill provides a truly traditional setting with original charm and character, and all the too-ing and fro-ing of an eclectic country house in the middle of the city.

Ruinart

Roast Cauliflower with Pistachio & Capers

The combination of toasted nutty pistachios, sweet golden raisins and cooling whipped tofu really elevates this humble brassica to be the proud star of any dinner table. - Head Chef, Allan McLaughlin.

Preparation time: 35 minutes | Cooking time: 15 minutes | Serves: 4

For the cauliflower
1 medium cauliflower
Salt and pepper, to season
1 tbsp dairy-free spread
2 sprigs of thyme

For the caper dressing
100ml cold pressed rapeseed oil
4 shallots, finely diced
50g capers, washed
50g golden raisins
1 tbsp chopped thyme
½ tbsp roughly chopped toasted pistachios

For the pistachio Romesco
50g peeled pistachios
50g flaked almonds
3 green peppers
1 clove of garlic
100ml olive oil
Sea salt

For the tofu whip
500g tofu
1 lemon, juiced
Sea salt

For the garnish
A mix of picked soft herbs like chervil, tarragon and dill

For the cauliflower

Remove the leaves, trim the base and steam for 10 minutes. Allow the cauliflower to cool down and slice into quarters. Preheat the oven to 180°c. Season the cauliflower with salt and pepper. Bring a heavy-based pan to a medium-high heat and sear the cauliflower on the cut sides. Add the dairy-free spread and thyme, then place in the oven to roast for 10-15 minutes.

For the caper dressing

Place the rapeseed oil and shallots into a small saucepan and gently warm on a very low heat until tender and opaque. Allow to cool, then add the remaining ingredients and mix to combine.

For the pistachio Romesco

Roast the pistachios and almonds slowly in the oven at 170°c for 8-10 minutes until evenly coloured, then allow to cool. Grill the peppers evenly until the skin blackens and blisters, then transfer to a bowl and cover tightly with a lid or cling film to steam. Deseed and remove the skin from the peppers, then place them in a blender with the toasted nuts, garlic and the olive oil. Blend until you have a fine purée, scraping down the sides of the bowl to ensure everything is well combined, then season with salt to taste.

For the tofu whip

Blend the tofu, lemon juice and sea salt (to taste) in a blender until smooth and creamy.

To serve

Start with a dollop of tofu whip on the plate, then a generous spoonful of the pistachio Romesco to follow. Place the roast cauliflower in the centre and drizzle with the caper dressing. Finally, garnish with a mix of picked soft herbs like chervil, tarragon and dill.

Good Honest Cooking

Freshly made food without the fuss is what you'll find at The Picnic Hamper, whether you drop in to the friendly café or sample their catering in and around Oxfordshire.

The Picnic Hamper in Monument Business Park outside Chalgrove, near Oxford, has been going strong for over 25 years. The popular café is also an outside caterer and wholesale supplier to various businesses in the education sector, known for the reliable and honest service from owner Debbie Warland and her team. Having worked for the same company over a long period of time and been head chef for Oxford University Press, Debbie decided to set up on her own doing what she knew best. Now with seven staff, The Picnic Hamper is still independently run by Debbie and her team who pride themselves on a friendly welcome and freshly made food for all.

The daily menu features a range of hot food including curries, lasagne and quiche alongside a salad bar, snacks and treats. Absolutely everything is homemade and cooked from scratch, even the sauces, in the onsite kitchen headed up by Lisa. Fresh ingredients are bought in from the same fruit and vegetable supplier Debbie has used since she started the business, with meat from Hedges and Supreme Sausages who are close enough for the produce to be walked from door to door! Debbie has always considered animal welfare, food miles and other sustainable options when sourcing produce and also uses recyclable or biodegradable packaging throughout the business.

The Picnic Hamper opens Monday to Friday for breakfast and lunch, serving sit down and takeaway options from 7:30 in the morning to 3 in the afternoon. The many regular customers are comprised of locals from the nearby village, tradespeople and others who work in the business park. "We make everything to high standards which are very consistent, so people know they can get good, homemade food here," says Debbie. "It also comes down to all our staff – I'm very lucky to have some wonderful local people who have been with us a long time."

The small venture Debbie began has expanded over the years to include much larger premises – a nerve-wracking step at the time, she notes, but one that turned out very well – and a wide range of clients who use the catering service. Whether you're after coffee and cake or a meal to set you up for the day, The Picnic Hamper has a bit of everything for everyone!

The Picnic Hamper
Café & Business Lounge
01865 891720
We buy local:
We buy local:
FRESH FRUIT + VEGETABLES -
BASKERVILLE - ABINGDON
BREAD ROLLS + PATISSERIE
CORNFIELD BAKERY - WHEATLEY
#SupportLocal

Falafel with Salad and Pitta

A lovely vegetarian recipe which is suitable all year round. It's one of our chef Lisa's favourite dishes being a vegetarian herself. This dish is flavoursome as well as filling for a snack or a main course with salad.

Preparation time: 45 minutes | Cooking time: 5 minutes | Serves: 4

For the falafel

400g tinned chickpeas
2 spring onions, finely chopped
2 dessertspoons plain flour
1 tsp ground cumin
1 lemon, zest only
½ tsp salt
Freshly ground black pepper
4 tsp olive oil

For the salad

½ cucumber, peeled and thinly sliced
1 round lettuce, washed and leaves torn
2 tomatoes, roughly chopped
1 lemon, juice only
3 tbsp olive oil

To serve

4 pitta breads
Plain yoghurt
Chilli sauce
Hummus

For the falafel

Put the chickpeas in a saucepan and mash with a potato masher until as smooth as possible (if you have a non-stick pan, use a plastic masher to protect the coating). Add the spring onions, flour, cumin, lemon zest, and salt. Season with lots of black pepper and mix well with a wooden spoon.

Using your hands, form the mixture into 6 equal-sized balls and flatten slightly. Put half the oil into a frying pan over a low heat. Add the falafel and cook for 4 minutes. Flip each one onto the other side and add the remaining oil to the pan. Cook for a further 3-4 minutes, or until golden brown and crisp on both sides.

For the salad

Put the cucumber, lettuce and tomatoes in a large bowl. Squeeze the juice of half the lemon into a small bowl, add a pinch of salt and pepper and, using a fork, whisk in the olive oil to make a dressing. Pour this over the salad and mix well.

To serve

When you're ready to plate up, lightly toast the pitta breads then carefully slice open along one side using a sharp knife. Arrange a little salad in each pitta, top with some of the falafel and add a squeeze of juice from the remaining lemon half. Add a spoonful of yoghurt, chilli sauce or hummus (or a bit of all three!) to your liking. Serve with the remaining salad alongside.

Bon Appétit!

This French bistro in the heart of Oxford has been serving its traditional specialities to loyal customers for over 25 years. They remain proudly independent and passionate about what they do.

Pierre Victoire is a rustic French bistro where the focus is on producing high quality, traditional dishes. Their long list of specialities includes moules-frites, escargot, bouillabaisse and pithivier (beautifully decorated, round, enclosed pies) as well as tart tatin, crème brulée and crepes for dessert among many other tempting treats. The prix fixe menus, which are all set at reasonable prices for two or three courses just as you would find in France, change every two to three months. They are based on fresh seasonal produce which is as locally sourced as possible.

Co-owner Claire works with the chefs to develop the menus at Pierre Victoire, as well as overseeing the general running of the restaurant with the help of her managers. Head chef Eli has been at the restaurant for a number of years, while Alicja and Lenka head up front of house. Pierre Victoire owners Claire Harvey and Gordon Jamieson opened the Little Clarendon Street bistro on July 4th 1996, and it remains independently owned to this day. The friendly team know many of their customers by name, around 80% of whom are local and regular diners at the Little Clarendon Street institution.

The restaurant is open every evening and Friday, Saturday and Sunday lunches, offering an intimate venue that works for any occasion, particularly first dates – some of which work out so well that they come back to celebrate their engagement! Designed to feel like a little corner of Paris, Pierre Victoire features rustic touches like wooden tables and chairs, blackboards and unfussy décor. The commitment to consistent, reliable, quality food and drink maintains the well-loved business' success and despite a tough stretch during the pandemic, Pierre Victoire has lost none of its shine. Claire says they are always "grateful to loyal customers who have supported us through the hard times, and always appreciate what we do'. Pierre Victoire is a gem in the heart of Oxford.

owned and family
run
We source our
meats locally
where we can and
we make all our
desserts
Bon Appetit
We are privately
owned and family
run
We source our
meats locally
where we can and
we make all our
desserts
Bon Appetit

Tartiflette du Maison

Tartiflette is a traditional French dish originating from the Alps, well known as a great après ski supper! Its main ingredients are potato and the infamous strong smelling reblochon cheese, local to the Savoyarde region. Traditionally it contains sautéed lardons but at Pierre Victoire we've adapted it to be one of our most popular vegetarian dishes by replacing them with red peppers or mushrooms.

Preparation time: 30 minutes | Cooking time: 30-40 minutes | Serves: 8

1kg floury potatoes (ideally King Edwards)

25g butter

2 large onions, peeled and sliced

2 shallots, peeled and sliced

3 cloves of garlic, crushed or finely chopped

3 red peppers, deseeded and finely sliced OR 200g mushrooms, sliced OR 3 leeks, sliced

325g reblochon (the best and smelliest you can get)

500ml double cream

Peel and thinly slice the potatoes, then par boil until tender but still firm. Depending on the potato type and thickness, about 7-10 minutes should suffice. Drain, rinse under cold water to stop the cooking and then drain again. Spread out on a cloth to dry.

In another pan, melt half the butter and lightly sweat off the onions and shallots until soft and just starting to brown. Be careful not to burn them. Add the garlic towards the end and sweat off quickly. Set the onion mixture aside and melt the remaining butter in the pan. Sauté your chosen vegetable until partially softened. Layer the potato slices with the onion mixture and sautéed vegetables in a lightly greased ovenproof dish (approximately 20cm square and 5cm deep is best) until half full. Slice the reblochon and layer half over the potato mixture. Finish layering up the potatoes, onions, and vegetables. Now top the tartiflette by laying the remaining reblochon slices in an attractive pattern if you can. Very lightly beat the cream so it's not lumpy and season well with salt and ground black pepper. If you like spice (though in France they would be horrified) you could add some chilli flakes or finely chopped fresh chilli to taste at this point.

Pour the cream over the potato mixture so it's all covered and finish by grinding over some more black pepper to taste. You're almost done! Pop the dish into a preheated oven at 180°c, ideally on a baking try in case it bubbles over, and cook for 30-40 minutes.

You know the tartiflette is done when it's bubbling and has a wonderfully golden crunchy gratinée top. Serve piping hot with a dressed green salad and cornichon on the side.

As for a wine recommendation, nothing would go better than a Pinot Blanc – from Alsace, of course – or a minerally Riesling. If you prefer red, perhaps go for a light style like Pinot Noir or Fluerie.

Chef's Tip: You can use any vegetable you love in this dish to replace the red pepper/leek/mushroom as long as it's not too watery. Tomatoes, for example, would make the finished dish too wet.

Mel Giedroyc, Actress, Comedian and Television Presenter

Ellen's Gorgeous Gluten-Free Pizza Wraps!

The joy of recipes is that you can pinch them, adapt them, and pass them off as your own. This delightful concoction came to me via one of my daughters' oldest friends. Ellen's a student and loves to make these pizza-wraps when she comes to stay with us. They are brilliant. So delicious, light, and dead easy to knock up. They are good if you're on a budget too. Here we go... (and if you're reading this, I owe you a glass of wine, Ellen!)

Prep time: 5 minutes | Cooking time: 5 minutes (20 if making own sauce) | Makes as many as you like

Gluten-free wraps (you should be able to find these in most supermarkets – some have seeds on which I like – or you can of course use normal wraps, but there's something really nice and light about the gluten-free ones)

Homemade tomato sauce (or if you haven't got time to make a tomato sauce then use a pre-made one from a jar. I certainly won't judge you...)

Pesto (from a jar or if you're feeling fancy, you can make your own)

Mozzarella, torn into chunks

Mushrooms

Basil leaves

Olives

If you are making your own tomato sauce, chuck a load of cherry tomatoes with lots of olive oil, salt, pepper, and crushed garlic into a pan. Simmer on a low heat and enjoy the FABULOUS AROMAS as it magically turns into a sauce over 20 minutes or so. It's quite useful to have a load of this in the fridge for all your tomato sauce eventualities.

Now for the wraps. This is really not rocket science. Which gets me thinking, you could add rocket here as well as basil. Lay your wraps out on a baking sheet. If you want to prepare all of your wraps at once then you can, or just do them as people ask for them: they're that quick and easy. Smear a goodly dollop of tomato sauce all over each wrap, then dot bits of pesto onto each one with a teaspoon, to taste. Sprinkle on chunks of mozzarella, mushrooms, basil, olives... whatever floats your boat to be honest. Go wild and experiment. Artichoke? Onion? Kimchi? Maybe not kimchi...

Place the wraps under a hot grill and watch like a hawk. You may be looking at 3-4 minutes on these little fellas. So keep a close eye. Oh dear, this is making me hungry – I'm just going to go to the fridge and see if we've got the correct ingredients...

P.S. I am a person who HAS to nap after lunch if I've eaten too many carbs. 18 minutes is usually ideal for this. I can honestly say (and I have conducted almost scientific-level experiments) that you categorically do NOT need to nap after eating one, two or even three of Ellen's Gorgeous Gluten-Free Pizza Wraps.

We are so pleased that Mel has once again contributed to our cookbook. Mel moved to Oxford when she was 11 and remembers coming to Sobell House with her mum, who volunteered at the hospice.

Homemade and From the Heart

Fresh ingredients, authentic recipes and a wide range of sweet and savoury vegan delights are the hallmarks of Pindy's Samosas, a small Oxfordshire-based producer with big flavour.

Since it was established in 2017, Pindy's Samosas has weathered the pandemic and come out the other side even stronger, having recently expanded into bigger product ranges and more markets to sell the incredibly popular home-cooked delights that give the business its name. Part of this success is down to owner Pindy Basan's commitment to doing things properly. She has been making samosas from a young age, taught by her mum who shared everything there is to know about Indian cooking with her daughters. Each samosa is made to perfection with specific processes that have been refined by Pindy to create the best possible combination of textures and flavours.

Customers can order various box sizes and sweet or savoury options of the artisan samosas through the website. Pindy even created a Biscoff special which has proven very popular! Her vegetable samosa is always a clear winner though, which draws on the tried and tested family recipe. Pindy also makes vegetable curries which can be enjoyed in her new curry wraps, which use soft fresh chapatis to create delicious handheld meals. Her aloo vada and pakora are great gluten-free options.

All Pindy's food is vegetarian and most is vegan, offering people with these dietary needs peace of mind thanks to a strictly meat-free and egg-free kitchen. Avoiding cross-contamination is very important to Pindy and she even uses seperate oils to fry each of the different samosa varieties. This careful approach is underpinned by an ethos that prioritises the purity of the product as well as avoiding harm to animals. Pindy's husband Surj is a strict vegan himself and so the products made in her kitchen are exactly what the family would eat at home, as authenticity is one of her key values.

This commitment to quality is what makes Pindy's Samosas special and so different from supermarket snacks and curries; she never takes shortcuts because her careful planning and attention to detail is crucial to getting each product right every time. Having begun by selling at markets in her local area, Pindy is now a regular stallholder at artisan markets across Oxford, Wantage, Didcot and Hungerford. She is as passionate as ever about creating the best possible home-cooked food and hopes to offer cooking classes in the future so more people can enjoy the art of making the perfect samosa!

Lotus

Butternut Squash Sabji

Butternut squash sabji is a north Indian dish. Its spicy and sweet flavour, together with a fragrant blend of spices, makes it a very popular vegan dish or side. It's best served with homemade chapati or rice. This recipe is vegan, gluten-free, quick and easy.

Preparation time: 10 minutes | Cooking time: 30-35 minutes | Serves: 2

1 butternut squash
1 red bell pepper
2 tbsp oil
2 tsp Panch Puran Five Spice (cumin, brown mustard, fenugreek, nigella and fennel)
1 medium onion, finely chopped
3 cloves of garlic, minced
1 tsp minced fresh ginger
1 green chilli, minced (can be deseeded for less heat, use more or less to taste)
½ tsp garam masala
½ tsp ground coriander
½ tsp mango powder
1 tsp ground turmeric
1 tsp red crushed chilli
1 tsp salt
1 tsp sugar
1 fresh tomato, finely diced
60ml water
2 tbsp chopped coriander

Peel the butternut squash, deseed and chop it into 1 inch pieces. Dice the red pepper and then temper in a hot pan for about 5 minutes until softened. Set aside.

Heat the oil in a wide pan and add the Panch Puran Five Spice. Once the seeds begin to crackle, add the onion and fry until translucent. Add the garlic, ginger and green chilli to fry for about 2 more minutes.

Add the spices (garam masala, ground coriander, mango powder, turmeric, red crushed chilli) along with the salt and sugar. Stir to combine everything and fry for about 2 minutes.

Now add the diced tomato and sauté until the tomato pieces are soft. Next, add the chopped butternut squash and mix well. Finally, add the water and cover the pan.

Cook the sabji over a low flame for about 5 minutes and then add the tempered red pepper. Cook everything further until the butternut squash pieces are tender and soft. Sprinkle the chopped coriander over the cooked sabji, mix and then turn off the heat.

Serve the sabji with either homemade roti or basmati rice.

Breaking New Ground

The Plough is a community-owned pub whose goal is to champion local farmers and local produce, as well as having a lot of fun along the way!

Owain and Luke took over the tenancy of this beautiful 16th century village pub in May 2022. Luke, being a local Hanney man, has a passion for supporting local produce, and Owain was brought up on a farm so wants to support as many local farmers as possible. With this ethos, they have created a pub that is not only a great place to eat but a local pub that caters for everyone. They believe that a pub is so important to the local community and want everyone to feel welcome, so whether you want to pop in for a pint after work or come for your 25th anniversary dinner, you will be welcomed with a big smile, a great pint of beer, and a beautiful plate of food.

The Plough serves up classic pub food – you can always get your favourite fish and chips, burgers, or sausages and mash – alongside some more adventurous options, such as rabbit keema and bone marrow with malt vinegar gel. The modern British menu is highly seasonal and uses locally sourced produce, including sausages from Owain's dad's farm! Luke and his sous chef Zico also use eggs from the farm next door and a local dairy farmer for ice cream amongst others. For those just after a pint, there's plenty of choice too, from Jeremy Clarkson's beer and cider to the five ales on tap that are brewed within 10 miles.

The Plough also works with two independent Oxfordshire wine suppliers, helping them curate a list of 'old world, new world, and out of this world' bottles that enable people to order their favourites or try something a little bit different. Owain, who manages front of house, is strongly committed to ensuring that this variety of choice applies across the board. "We just want to make sure that people are comfortable coming here in muddy boots or dressed up for a fancy dinner," he says. The clean-cut but traditionally decked out interiors give The Plough a proper village pub feel, and they have already made Ox In A Box's Top 50 Pub Gardens in Oxfordshire for the outdoor space. Despite having been open for such a short time, they are already settling into the heart of the community, just where a true pub belongs.

THE PLOUGH
at West Hanney
OMMUNITY
FREE HOUSE

Plough Bhaji Burger

This hearty meal takes the flavours of the much-loved Indian snack and combines them in a delicious vegan burger. Served with coriander yoghurt and Bombay Aloo chips, this is a real summer sizzler.

Preparation time: 45-50 minutes | Cooking time: 15 minutes | Serves: 2

4 carrots
1 fennel bulb
2 shallots
1 bunch of fresh coriander
2 tbsp curry powder
5g caraway seeds
5g cumin seeds
Salt and pepper
150g gram flour
100ml vegan yoghurt
2 vegan brioche burger buns

Grate the carrots, finely slice the fennel and shallots, then combine the veg in a large mixing bowl. Roughly chop the fresh coriander and add half to the bowl with half the curry powder.

Toast the seeds in a dry pan, then add them to the bowl along with 2 generous pinches of salt. Stir in the gram flour until everything is combined, then cover the bowl with cling film and leave in the fridge for 30 minutes. Meanwhile, preheat the oven to 180°c.

Take the burger mix out the fridge and form into 2 large patties. Shallow fry the patties for 2 minutes on each side until golden brown, then place in the preheated oven for 10 minutes to cook through.

Stir the remaining chopped coriander into the vegan yoghurt and season to taste with salt and pepper. We use a coriander oil to split the yoghurt but chopped has just the same effect.

Toast the buns, add a generous spoonful of coriander yoghurt to the base and place the bhaji burger on top. Serve with a pot of coriander yoghurt and some Bombay Aloo chips on the side.

Be Our Guest

You can chat to the cook in the kitchen and enjoy delicious food in the cosy dining room, but at The Secret Supper Society you won't be paying restaurant prices or doing the washing up!

The Secret Supper Society was established over fifteen years ago, in a lightbulb moment for keen cook Jules. She came across the concept of hosting dinner for strangers at home while researching recipes, and instantly knew it was something she wanted to try. Three weeks later, her first evening went down a treat, and the venture took off very quickly as one of the UK's first supper clubs.

"I'm not a trained chef but I've always loved hosting dinner parties, so for me this was a natural progression that allowed a more artistic approach," says Jules.

The five or six course meals are hosted in the comfortable dining room of her farmhouse in North Oxfordshire, and always book up well in advance. Menus draw inspiration from a wide range of cuisines; Jules is motivated by the seasons and amazing local produce including cultured butter by artisan producer Grant Harrington, fresh loaves of sourdough bread from Forge House Bakery, and top quality meat supplied by Farmison & Co in Yorkshire. "I eat and sleep food, have a million cook books, and jot down new ideas constantly," she explains. "It's a full-time job to plan the courses around complementary flavour profiles, order ingredients, create a beautiful setting and prepare every element from scratch (down to the crackers for cheese and chocolates to finish) not least because I'm a complete perfectionist!"

Paying attention to the details within such a homely setting allows diners to experience a unique marriage of restaurant quality food, plus their own drinks with no corkage charge, and the relaxed atmosphere of a dinner party with friends. Jules and her husband Nick — who created The Secret Supper Society's branding and menu database (so that returning guests never have the same meal twice, unless they request it!) and is also the waiter — find that people love the element of surprise in not knowing what they'll be served, and often try things they would never have ordered but discover delicious new dishes in the process. The Secret Supper Society also offers the chance to try many of these dishes from the comforts of home, as Jules has collated nearly 400 recipes on the website which includes over 100 free recipes in the BBC section.

Since Covid, Jules has bagged herself a regular Tuesday afternoon slot on BBC Radio Oxford, so make sure to give her a listen! She's also hosted woodland pop-ups and a pop-up picnic, outdoor variations of her usual supper club, and previously donated dinners to Sobell House through a silent auction. Her flexibility as a one-woman enterprise has enabled The Secret Supper Society to thrive, bringing joy to adventurous foodies thanks to Jules' talent and genuine passion for welcoming guests to her 'home from home' restaurant.

SOCIETY
Ricotta with & Confit Tomatoes
on Toasted Ciabatta
Marinated Tomatoes with Burrata
& Balsamic Pearls
Beetroot Salad on Rye Bread with
Smoked Salmon
Beef Fillet, Bearnaise Sauce, Watercress
& Cloud Potatoes
Cheese Course
Lemon Verbena Panna Cotta & Shortbread
Recipes available
on my website
Scan me for free
30 day trial.
SMIRNOFF
EG
TWININGS
OF LONDON

Pasta Pie

A great dish to make with children; no sharp knives, easy to make and their sense of achievement when it comes out of the oven will be enormous. There are certainly easier ways to make pasta, tomato, and cheese but this is impressive and great to share with friends!

Preparation time: 10 minutes, plus 15 minutes resting | Cooking time: 1 hour | Serves: 6

3 tbsp olive oil
300g rigatoni pasta
750g marinara sauce (shop-bought is fine)
100g ricotta
10 basil leaves
125g mozzarella, torn into pieces
100g parmesan, grated

Preheat the oven to 190°c fan. Line a baking tray with foil and grease a 20cm springform cake tin with 1 tablespoon of the olive oil.

Bring a large pan of salted water to the boil and cook the rigatoni for 8 minutes until only just al dente. Drain into a bowl, toss with the remaining oil, and leave to cool a little.

Stand the rigatoni up in the cake tin until the base is fully covered. Put the cake tin on the lined baking tray. Pour over the marinara sauce using a spatula or the back of a spoon to caress the sauce into the tubes. Smear the top with ricotta, dot with basil leaves, then sprinkle over the mozzarella and the parmesan. Cover with foil and bake for 30 minutes.

Remove the foil and bake for a further 20 minutes. Remove from the oven and allow to rest for 15 minutes before releasing the pie from the outside edge of the cake tin.

Paul Chahidi, Actor and Sobell Charity Ambassador

Aklima's Epic Bengali Dhal

I was first made this dish by my very good friend Jason Hill, who is the best amateur chef I know. He was taught it by Aklima, a Bangladeshi refugee now turned part-time cookery instructor. It's authentic, easy to make and most importantly, it's truly delicious. The twist is to fry and add the garlic (and some lemon juice) at the end of the cooking process, which gives the dish an incredible flavour and a deliciously creamy texture. You won't be able to stop eating it!

Preparation time: 10 minutes | Cooking time: 30-35 minutes | Serves: 4 as a main or 6 as a side dish

- 3 onions, sliced
- 2 tbsp vegetable oil
- 750g red lentils
- 2 fresh tomatoes, grated
- 2 bay leaves
- 1 tbsp salt
- 1 tbsp curry powder
- 1 tsp ground turmeric
- 1 lemon, juiced
- 1 whole garlic bulb, peeled and thinly sliced
- 65g ghee (or butter)
- 20g fresh coriander, roughly chopped

Gently fry the onions in half the vegetable oil on a medium-low heat, for about 10 minutes, until they are translucent and just starting to turn golden brown.

Wash the lentils until the water runs clear and then add them to 1 litre of boiling water in a saucepan. Add the cooked onions, grated tomatoes, bay leaves, salt, curry powder, turmeric, and half the lemon juice. Leave to simmer for 25 minutes, stirring occasionally to stop it sticking to the pan.

Using a potato masher, mash the mixture together until it makes a thick paste. You may need to add a little more water (up to a cup full).

Now, in a separate frying pan on a medium heat, fry the sliced garlic in the ghee and remaining vegetable oil. You want the garlic to turn a nice golden brown, but be careful not to burn it, as it can catch quickly towards the end. Add the fried garlic to the dhal and give it a good stir to mix well. Add the remaining lemon juice, give it a quick stir, then sprinkle over the chopped coriander.

Serve your dhal with rice, or with a fluffy naan.

Paul grew up in Summertown, Oxford, and has had a personal connection to Sobell House since his father was cared for by the hospice in 2015.

Breakfast, Lunch and Tee

Studley Wood Golf Club offers a café-culture dining experience in the heart of Oxfordshire; the restaurant opens its doors to not only the club's members but to everyone.

Situated in the beautiful Oxfordshire countryside on the edge of Horton Cum Studley village is an eatery which has become the hot spot for the locals: Studley Wood Golf Club. The privately owned, family-run business was established almost 25 years ago and the team at Studley Wood are a close-knit family themselves, making the experience a familiar and friendly one for their customers. Not only are they offering tasty food in Oxfordshire, but great service and of course a game of golf too.

From salads to paninis, Studley Wood has a range of breakfast and lunch options to be enjoyed in the beautiful surroundings, complete with a patio and balcony area. Produce is sourced from local suppliers including the Natural Bread Company for bread, cakes, and other treats. The venue also hosts events including the annual Sobell House golf day, which starts with the staple golfers' breakfast of coffee and bacon rolls, followed by 18 holes and a two-course lunch. Studley Wood is a great place to celebrate and regularly hosts birthday parties, functions, and evening events.

The restaurant at Studley Wood prides itself on a welcoming experience for all, thanks to the homely atmosphere and café-culture feel. Whether it's a meet up with friends or a peaceful work-from-home spot, the relaxed and comfortable environment means their customers won't want to leave! The licensed venue boosts the atmosphere as people come to get a taste of renowned casque mark real ales and bean to cup coffee.

Determined to showcase the business and their hidden gem, Studley Wood has recently hosted the PGA EuroPro Tour, televised on Sky, as well as recently being featured on BBC's The One Show. The aim is to put Studley Wood Golf Club on the map and uncover the beauty of this sporting and dining experience in the country.

STUDLEY WOOD
GOLF CLUB

Zingy Lentil and Halloumi Salad

We rely on local suppliers to provide us with the best seasonal and locally sourced ingredients. Our golfers and visitors like fresh and easy to eat lunches, with this recipe being a favourite light lunch during the warmer summer months.

Preparation time: 10 minutes | Cooking time: 2 minutes | Serves: 4

820g cooked green lentils, refreshed under cold water
2 heads of chicory, trimmed and leaves separated
300g cherry tomatoes, halved
300g light vegetarian halloumi, sliced into 16
1 tbsp extra virgin olive oil
2 spring onions, finely sliced
Fresh oregano leaves, to garnish

For the dressing
4 tbsp extra virgin olive oil
4 tbsp wholegrain mustard
3 tbsp roughly chopped capers
2 tbsp white wine vinegar
1 lemon, zested and juiced
1 heaped tbsp oregano

Whisk all the ingredients for the dressing together in a bowl and season well.

Tip the lentils into a sieve and rinse with a kettle full of hot water, then drain well. Tip into a bowl and mix with half the dressing.

Toss the chicory leaves and cherry tomatoes with the rest of the dressing.

Heat a large non-stick frying pan over a medium heat. Toss the halloumi slices with the olive oil, then fry for approximately 1 minute until golden brown.

Add the halloumi to the chicory and tomatoes, making sure all the ingredients are coated in the dressing.

Divide the lentils between 4 salad bowls and top with the dressed halloumi, chicory and tomatoes. Garnish with the finely sliced spring onions and a few fresh oregano leaves.

Happy Everest After...

Taste Tibet is on a mission to put Tibetan food on the culinary map, and with a restaurant and takeaway, festival food stall and new cookbook, owners Yeshi and Julie are well on their way to achieving that goal.

The story of Taste Tibet begins on the Tibetan Plateau where Yeshi Jampa grew up. He followed the nomadic lifestyle of his family, learning to cook over a fire inside a yak hair tent at a young age. When he was 19, Yeshi walked across the Himalayas to northern India, where he lived for many years and later met Julie Kleeman on her own travels. Now settled in the UK with two children, Yeshi and Julie have developed a unique business venture that showcases the warming, homely, flavourful delights of authentic Tibetan cooking in Oxford and beyond.

Taste Tibet started out in 2014 as a street food stall at local markets, events and festivals. Owners Yeshi and Julie also ran a takeaway from their own home in east Oxford. In November 2020 they opened the Taste Tibet restaurant and takeaway, which also offers home-cooked food for the freezer. Taste Tibet has an informal, neighbourhood feel that stays true to their roots. Despite launching mid-lockdown, Yeshi and Julie never worried that the restaurant wouldn't work because of the huge amount of local support that Taste Tibet has enjoyed over the years. Locals are hooked on Yeshi's delicious stews, curries, stir fries and momos (irresistible Tibetan dumplings), and many of the people dining at Taste Tibet today have been customers since the earliest days.

Yeshi and Julie have woven a semi-nomadic lifestyle into their new livelihood by continuing to take their Tibetan tent to festivals including Hay, Latitude and Glastonbury over the summer months. "Food is such a fantastic lens into another culture," says Julie. "We love having conversations with people who have never heard of momos or eaten Tibetan food before. It's quite hard to come by in the UK and we want to share it with as many people as possible." To this end, Yeshi and Julie also wrote the Taste Tibet cookbook, published by Murdoch Books in 2022. Their book features family recipes and stories from Yeshi's childhood in Tibet, as well as the secrets to making all the dishes that have made them the thriving independent business that they are today.

The Taste Tibet menu features dishes that Yeshi learnt to cook by watching family members huddled around the family hearth or out in their nomadic tents. Despite these uniquely Tibetan origins, the culture of working with whatever you have to hand in a harsh landscape means that most recipes are very flexible and adaptable, using vegetables, spices and other ingredients that can easily can be found in supermarkets across the UK...except for yak milk and meat which is not so readily available here! With a shared passion for food and wellbeing, Yeshi and Julie bring their memories and experiences to life through Taste Tibet.

TASTE TIBET
TASTE TIBET
We are Time Out's Best Restaurant in Oxford rig now and 2021 Best Takea finalists (BBC Food Awards
Our opening times are :
Lunch Menu
TASTE TIBET
TASTE TIBET
HIMALAYAN SOUL FOOD

Mixed Vegetable Creamy Coconut Curry

In Tibet - and in India, where he lived for many years - Yeshi found it impossible to get vegetables that were out of season. When he first arrived in the UK, he found it fascinating that the markets and shops stocked the same fruit and veg all year round, regardless of the season. However, he soon grew weary of the sameness of fruit and vegetable shopping here on this small island and has since found it one of the hardest things to get used to. Happily, as the years have gone by, and through the contacts we've made with wholesalers for our restaurant and festival stall, we've found ways of accessing fresh, local, seasonal produce and we always try to cook with it when we can. If you'd like to do the same, feel free to substitute the courgette with pumpkin in autumn or the cauliflower with peppers in summer, and so on.

Preparation time: 10 minutes | Cooking time: 40 minutes | Serves: 4-6

4cm root ginger, washed but not peeled
4 large cloves of garlic
1 red onion
2 large tomatoes
2 tbsp cooking oil
¼ tsp ground turmeric
1 tsp Bassar curry masala (or hot chilli powder)
2 tsp Madras curry powder
400ml coconut milk
9 baby potatoes (about 400g)
2 carrots (about 250g)
½ cauliflower (about 350g)
1 courgette (about 250g)
2 tsp salt
3 tbsp coconut milk powder (optional)
Chopped coriander, including stems (optional)

Finely chop the ginger, garlic, onion and tomatoes. Make sure everything is very small, as this will form the base of your curry paste. Put the oil into a large wok and place over a medium-high heat. When hot, add the ginger and garlic and stir fry until golden, then add the onion and stir fry for about 2 minutes. Stir in the tomatoes, turmeric, curry masala and curry powder and mix thoroughly into the paste. Now turn the heat up as high as it will go and add the coconut milk. Stir well, and then cook for 15 minutes, stirring occasionally.

Meanwhile, cut the rest of the vegetables into bite-sized pieces (the cauliflower pieces can be a little larger than the others). Put the potatoes and carrots into one bowl, as these will go in first, and the cauliflower and courgette in another. Add the salt, potatoes and carrots to the wok along with the coconut milk powder, if using. Pour in 100ml of boiling water and stir well, then turn the heat down to low-medium, cover and leave to simmer for about 10 minutes, stirring occasionally.

Now add the cauliflower and courgette. If the sauce looks a bit dry, add another splash of boiling water. Cook, stirring every so often, for a further 7-8 minutes, or until all the vegetables are tender. Garnish the curry with fresh coriander, if using, and serve with basmati rice.

Recipe originally published in Taste Tibet by Julie Kleeman and Yeshi Jampa, published by Murdoch Books.

A Source of Inspiration

Built on a strong ethos of sourcing and supporting local, The Tite Inn has transformed a village pub into a destination for fantastic food and drink.

The team behind Chadlington Brewery jumped at the opportunity to take on new challenges in the lockdown of 2021 when a local pub came up for sale. Despite the short time The Tite Inn has been in their hands, they have already undertaken a complete refurbishment and change of menu in line with their core values. "It's very important to us that we stay connected with the area and support other local businesses," explains managing director of the pub and brewery, Jason Chipchase. "We pride ourselves on sourcing as local and fresh as possible, creating a great experience for our guests and offering value for money too, without costing the earth."

The Tite Inn's food is always fresh, seasonal, and full of ingredients from nearby producers and suppliers. These include Pudlicote Farm for meat and vegetables, situated next door to the pub, and Salt Pig Oxfordshire cured meats. A large section of the menu is vegan and vegetarian, and dishes change seasonally depending on what's available. Alongside the core menu, the specials board acts almost like another menu in itself with exciting new dishes being developed all the time, offering customers a great range of options all year round. Head chef Jimmy Keen works with Jason and general manager Callum Jefferies to align the food and drink offering between pub and brewery.

Tite is an old Oxfordshire word for water source, so it was the perfect name for a pub serving beers brewed with the local spring water. As part of their environmentally conscious ethos, Chadlington Brewery also works with Bruern Farm and Estate, who produce grains untouched by chemicals, and are the only brewery in the UK to brew with an ancient native barley grown with regenerative farming practices. This is used in their Oxford Heritage, one of the wide range of beers (mostly gluten-free) that are all designed to celebrate Oxfordshire and the Cotswolds.

The pub also works in collaboration with Oxford Wines, who source and recommend new wines as well as training The Tite Inn's front of house team to ensure all the staff are equipped with extensive knowledge. Customers can enjoy their choice of beer, wine, gin and of course a delicious lunch or evening meal in the cosy interior or the beautiful garden. Whatever the time of year, there will always be something new for everyone at The Tite Inn, underpinned by a commitment to quality produce that looks after nature and showcases the best of its idyllic countryside setting.

THE TITE
INN
BOAT RACE
BOATRACE
CHADLINGTON
OXFORD
BLUE
CHADLINGTON
OXFORD
IPA
CHADLINGTON
OXFORD
HERITAGE

Ratatouille Risotto with Rocket Pesto

This delicious dish is a fusion of rustic French and Italian classics, with the addition of a vibrant rocket pesto, peppery raw radish and tangy goat's cheese to freshen up the flavours.

Preparation time: 10 minutes | Cooking time: 20 minutes | Serves: 2

For the rocket pesto
50g pine nuts
50g parmesan
100g rocket
150ml olive oil
1 clove of garlic

For the risotto
1 onion, diced
2 cloves of garlic, crushed
2 tbsp olive oil
2 courgettes, diced
1 aubergine, diced
1 red pepper, diced
200g risotto rice
500ml vegetable stock
2 tsp tomato purée
1 radish, finely sliced
20g goat's cheese, crumbled

For the rocket pesto

Toast the pine nuts under a grill. Be careful as they burn easily. Allow to cool. Place all the ingredients into a food blender and mix for 1 minute. Add salt and pepper to taste.

For the risotto

Gently cook the diced onion and crushed garlic in the olive oil until softened. Add the diced vegetables and cook for a further 5 minutes until softened.

Add the risotto rice to the pan and stir to coat all the grains in oil. Slowly add the hot vegetable stock a ladle at a time, continuously stirring the risotto.

Once all the stock has been added and the rice is swollen and cooked, add the tomato purée. Continue to stir until the purée is all mixed in.

Remove the risotto from the heat and season to taste with salt and pepper. To serve, portion the risotto into bowls of your choice. Carefully place some sliced radish on top of the risotto, sprinkle with the crumbled goat's cheese and finish with small dots of the rocket pesto.

Rick Stein, Chef, Restaurateur, Writer and Television Presenter

Whole Eggs in Coconut Masala

I really wanted to contribute a recipe to Sobell House Hospice, who cared for my brother John Stein's research colleague, Colin Blakemore, of whom I was a great admirer.

Preparation time: 5 minutes | Cooking time: 10-15 | Serves: 4

3 tbsp mustard oil or vegetable oil
6 hard-boiled free-range eggs, peeled and left whole
1 tsp turmeric
1 tsp Kashmiri chilli powder
400ml coconut milk
2 medium red onions, very thinly sliced
20g fresh ginger, finely shredded
3 fresh green chillies, thinly sliced, with seeds
½ tsp salt
1 tsp sugar
Handful of coriander leaves, chopped
½ tsp garam masala (see method)
350g long-grain or basmati rice
600ml water

Heat the oil in a heavy-based saucepan or karahi over a medium heat, add the whole eggs and fry for 1-2 minutes until lightly coloured, then add the turmeric and chilli powder and cook for another 30 seconds. Stir in the coconut milk and bring to a simmer.

Add the onions, ginger, chillies and salt. Simmer for 5 minutes until the coconut milk has reduced in volume by half and the onions are just softened, adding a splash of water if it becomes too thick. Stir in the sugar and coriander, then sprinkle with garam masala. Halve the eggs just before serving.

Put the rice into a 20cm heavy-based saucepan and add the water. Quickly bring to the boil, stir once, cover with a tight-fitting lid, reduce the heat to low and cook for 10–15 minutes. I cook my rice for only 10 minutes as I like a very slight firmness to the grain. Simmer for 12–15 minutes if you like a softer texture. Once done to your liking, uncover the pan, fluff up the grains with a fork, and serve with the egg molee.

To make your own garam masala

This is my own garam masala recipe, which is essentially a balanced combination of the most popular spices. Even more important than the mix is having them freshly roasted and ground. I can't stress too strongly how much better it is to make your own garam masala than to buy it. This mixture represents perfect balance to me. It's important to make this regularly; I would suggest renewing it every month.

(makes 50g)
1 tbsp black peppercorns
2 tbsp cumin seeds
2 tbsp coriander seeds
2 tsp cardamom seeds (from 30–40 green pods)
4 tsp whole cloves
7cm piece of cinnamon stick
1 whole nutmeg

Roast all the spices apart from the nutmeg in a dry frying pan over a medium heat for a couple of minutes until toasted and aromatic. Cool. Grate the nutmeg and add to a spice grinder along with the whole spices (you might want to break up the cinnamon stick) and grind everything to a fine powder. Store in a sealed container out of the sunlight. It will keep its most aromatic condition for a month.

Reproduced by kind permission of BBC Books, first published in Rick Stein's India 2013

Hospitality at Hart

The White Hart in Fyfield is a charming country dining pub that puts great food and hospitality at its heart. Often described as a foodie's paradise, it is a hub for both locals and visitors to gather, feast, relax and make memories.

Since arriving at the White Hart in 2005, Mark and Kay Chandler have restored this beautiful hostelry to its 15th century former glory. From the vaulted ceiling to the minstrel's gallery, this unique space is steeped in history. As a family-run business, everything here is done with care, thought and passion and the impressive list of awards is testament to this.

"Mark and I fell in love with the White Hart when we first saw it and we are still passionate about what we do 17 years on," explains Kay. "We are proud to be independent and support our community. We love the fact we grow our own produce and prepare everything fresh. We love that we make people happy. Quite simply, we have created the sort of experience that we like when we go out to eat."

The pub's modern British dishes are developed according to what's growing in the pub's kitchen garden and the surrounding countryside, as well as what's available on foraging expeditions. Mark heads up the culinary team; he began cooking when they took the pub on and were looking for chefs but no one they found was as good, so he decided to continue in that role. A year later The White Hart was awarded two AA rosettes for culinary excellence and he has never looked back!

By working with local farmers and suppliers alongside homegrown produce, new dishes can be created daily using the freshest seasonal ingredients. "This involves a lot of prep and is time consuming," says Mark, "but it's exciting for us and for the customers. They want to come back and see what is new, and our chefs are motivated by the creative opportunities."

Having said that, there's one dish that simply cannot be taken off the menu: the slow-roasted belly pork served with a foot long stick of crackling has become The White Hart's signature, and literally turns heads when brought through the dining room! Of course, being a village pub, you can simply wander in for a pint as the locals do or enjoy a bite in the new outdoor dining space complete with wood-fired pizza oven.

Kay and her team are committed to making sure every visit, whether it's a sit-down meal or a drink, is a wonderful experience for all their customers. From the warm welcome to the attention to detail, they do their utmost to ensure that each moment of your experience really hits the mark.

SOBELL
HOUSE
2016

Stuffed Tempura Courgette Flower with Summer Veg

This recipe symbolises our whole ethos of supporting local, sustainability and striving for zero food miles. We grow most of the ingredients ourselves in our kitchen garden and every mouthful is a taste of summer!

Preparation time: 45 minutes | Cooking time: 15 minutes | Serves: 4

For the pea puree
200g peas
Small sprig of mint & a pinch of sugar

For the courgette flowers
4 courgette flowers (stamens removed) with baby courgettes attached
400g ricotta & 50g pine nuts, toasted
50g parmesan, grated
1 bunch of basil & 1 lemon, zested

For the summer vegetables
1 courgette, 1cm diced
½ bulb of fennel, thinly sliced
100g chanterelle mushrooms, cleaned with a pastry brush
100g fine beans, 1cm diced, blanched
12 cherry tomatoes
8 spears of tender stem broccoli, blanched
Handful of peas and/or broad beans (without skins)
250ml vegetable stock
100g unsalted butter, cold and diced
12 cooked, cooled & halved new potatoes
5g each of fresh parsley, tarragon and chervil, chopped

For the tempura batter
150g plain flour & 50g cornflour
Pinch of baking powder
Small bottle of soda water (cold)
Vegetable or sunflower oil for deep frying
Pea shoots, to garnish (optional)

For the pea puree

Remove the mint leaves from their stems. Place the mint stems and peas in boiling water and cook for 3 minutes. Remove the peas and blend with the mint leaves, sugar, salt, pepper and a little of the cooking water, for about 1 minute. Add more water to achieve the desired consistency (a thick smooth purée). Pass through a fine sieve. Reserve until required.

For the courgette flowers and the summer vegetables

Combine the ricotta, pine nuts, parmesan, basil and lemon zest until well mixed. Transfer to a piping bag, pipe the filling into the courgette flowers and then refrigerate until needed. Sauté the courgette, fennel and mushrooms for 1 minute. Add the rest of the vegetables and the stock, then reduce the liquid by half. While this is still boiling, stir in the butter. Add the cooked potatoes and the fresh herbs. Season to taste.

For the tempura batter

Combine 100g of the plain flour with the cornflour and baking powder. Gradually whisk soda water into this mixture until you have a batter with the consistency of milk.

To cook the courgette flowers

Lightly dust the courgette flowers in the remaining 50g of flour. Dip the courgette and flower into the tempura batter and then gently drop into a deep fryer with the oil at 180°c for 2-3 minutes. Remove from the fryer and drain. The batter should be light and crispy.

To serve

Place the summer vegetables on the plate and the tempura courgette flower on top. Swipe the pea purée artistically on the plate. Garnish with pea shoots if desired.

An English Idyll

The White Hart of Wytham is often described as a hidden gem in the quintessentially English village of Wytham, not far from Oxford, for its freshly prepared food and cosy indoor or summery outdoor dining opportunities.

The White Hart of Wytham has a long history of welcoming guests and wetting whistles, being housed in a 16th century building, and there are records of a pub in the village dating back to 1741, but that was only when the records began! In more recent times, the pub has been under new management since January 2015 and offers more substantial fare to satisfy all appetites. "We're extremely proud and grateful to have received numerous awards and nominations for our food," says Mark Butcher, better known as Baz, the pub's current landlord.

Located a country mile from Oxford city centre, The White Hart is family and dog friendly, boasting two dining rooms, a large bar area, a conservatory, a beautiful secluded courtyard, an outdoor bar, and a renovated Georgian stable turned party room: you'll be spoilt for choice when deciding where to eat or drink and it's lucky that this popular destination also has a very large car park! In 2020, a number of beautiful gypsy caravan style dining pods were added to the courtyard, so small groups can dine out together under fairy lights in an intimate setting. In 2021, a large clear-roofed all-weather structure was installed over the courtyard – known as the Observatory – to provide year-round alfresco dining.

Food is always prepared and cooked from scratch on a daily basis at the pub, with the kitchen team using local suppliers wherever possible. You can often find Wytham Woods venison on the menu and there is also a full vegan and vegetarian menu that has garnered its own awards. The White Hart can cater for all types of events too, whether it's a wedding reception, afternoon tea or birthday party with exclusive hire or group reservations. Whatever the season or time of year, the pub offers a very hospitable welcome. In the winter there are roaring open log fires and woodburning stoves for extra warmth. In the summer al fresco eating and drinking is hard to beat, amidst the sounds of church bells and swallows, and the appetising aromas from the wood-fired asado barbecue in the courtyard.

Nestled in its lovely village location, The White Hart of Wytham is a place to enjoy award-winning food and drink just a stone's throw from the city in a quiet, unspoilt and historic setting.

The
WHITE
HART

Roasted Red Pepper Gnocchi, Smoked Garlic & Basil Espuma, Parmesan Crisp

This is a wonderful all-year-round vegetarian dish, suitable as a starter or a main course.

Preparation time: 1 hour | Cooking time: 20 minutes | Serves: 4-6

For the gnocchi
4 large red skinned potatoes
2 large Anaheim peppers or similar red point peppers
500g '00' flour
2 eggs and 2 egg yolks
Sea salt flakes
Black pepper
80g finely grated parmesan or Pecorino cheese

For the espuma foam
100g fresh basil leaves
1 shallot, peeled and diced
½ bulb of smoked garlic
500ml double cream
80g parmesan, grated

For the parmesan crisp
100g finely grated parmesan

For the gnocchi

Bake the potatoes whole for 90 minutes at 180°c until the skin is crisp and the centre is soft and fluffy. Meanwhile, roast the peppers whole over a naked flame until the skin is blackened and charred. Place the peppers into a sealed container to let the skin sweat off. Put the flour into a large bowl and make a well in the centre. In a separate bowl, whisk the eggs and yolks together, adding salt and pepper for seasoning. Halve the baked potatoes and scoop out the centres, discarding the skins. Peel and finely dice the charred peppers. Add the peppers and egg mixture to the well in the flour, then gradually bring everything together with your fingertips. Mix in the potato and the cheese, then shape the gnocchi dough into a rough ball and place in a floured bowl. Cover and place in the fridge for 30 minutes. Flour a clean surface and put a large pan of salted water on to boil. Roll out the chilled dough into a large sausage shape with the same diameter as a wine bottle neck, then cut into 1 inch pieces using the back of a knife. Add half to the pan of boiling water, cook for roughly 6 minutes or until the gnocchi pieces float, then transfer to iced water. Repeat with the second batch.

For the espuma foam

Blanch the basil in boiling water for 20 seconds, then transfer to iced water. Fry the shallot with the garlic until translucent on a medium heat. In another pan, boil the cream and reduce by one third. Blend the cream, shallot and garlic on a high speed for 2 minutes. Add the parmesan and seasoning to taste, then blitz again. Remove the basil from the water and squeeze out the moisture on a tea towel. Add to the blender and blitz for a further 5 minutes, until you have a bright green creamy sauce.

For the parmesan crisp

Line a baking tray with greaseproof paper. Spread out a fine layer of grated parmesan and place in the oven at 180°c for 10 minutes. Remove and leave to cool.

To serve

Remove the gnocchi from the iced water and place on paper towels. Heat a large frying pan with some olive oil and sauté the gnocchi for 3 minutes on both sides until browned, then divide evenly between serving plates. Gently heat the espuma in a pan, then use a stick blender or whisk to make the sauce frothy. Use a spoon to scoop off the foam and add it to the gnocchi. Serve with the parmesan crisp.

Roger Allam, Actor

Peperonata

I've only just discovered the cooking of this dish, though I must have eaten it on many occasions. It can be a pasta sauce, a side dish, or a condiment. Here is my current version of it. This recipe makes quite a lot, so halve the quantities if it's only for two of you, but it keeps well in the fridge for a week or so.

Preparation time: 10 minutes | Cooking time: 30-40 minutes (20 if making own sauce) | Serves: 2-4

1 good sized onion
5 peppers of all the colours
1 clove of garlic
2-3 tbsp olive oil
1 x 400g tin of tomatoes
Dried chilli or cayenne, to taste
Salt and black pepper

First, chop the onion and slice the peppers. Peel and finely chop the garlic, then set aside.

In a wide-bottomed chef's pan or casserole, stew the chopped onion in the olive oil until soft. This takes 10 minutes or so. Add the sliced peppers and cover the pan until they are well on the way to being cooked, for another 10 minutes or so.

While they are cooking, add the garlic and some dried chilli, cayenne pepper or however you like to add heat to food. Stir in the tinned tomatoes and let them stew until the oil separates from them and the mixture becomes pleasingly jammy.

You can add some chopped parsley at this stage if you wish, and season the peperonata to taste with salt and black pepper.

It's really nice as a pasta sauce, side dish or condiment so you can serve this however you like.

Many of us will recognise Roger as Oxford's Detective Inspector Fred Thursday in the drama series Endeavour, a prequel to the long-running Inspector Morse series. Roger is a good friend of Paul Chahidi, our Sobell Charity Ambassador.

Italian Food with a Twist

Founded in 2015 by Nick and Teo, White Rabbit are an Italian food company based in Chalgrove, Oxfordshire. They specialise in creating delicious gluten-free and plant-based products, all inspired by Teo's roots in Italia! From pizzas to ravioli, they do it all while supplying some of the UK's biggest supermarkets.

The challenger brand was born when Nick Croft-Simon met Italian pizza maestro Matteo Ferrari while working at The White Rabbit Pub, in Oxford, where Teo worked in the kitchen and Nick pulled the pints. Using chef Teo's generations of experience, passed to him via his family pizzeria in Bergamo, the entrepreneurial duo started refining and marketing authentic Italian-style thin and crispy pizzas off the pub's menu.

Within two years The White Rabbit was rated the number one pizzeria in Oxford on TripAdvisor, selling over 2000 pizzas a week. When customers started requesting gluten-free and dairy-free options, the boys were determined that these alternatives would be an added benefit without compromising the delicious taste their pizzas had become renowned for.

With a firm belief that everyone should be able to eat delicious pizza, they began sourcing the best tasting ingredients from all over the world, crafting an authentic gourmet gluten-free pizza, with a range of vegan options, that can be enjoyed by all.

The quality, taste and freshness that initially made the pizzas such a hit on The White Rabbit pub menu have gone on to win a range of awards and national listings as a brand in major retailers, as well as specialist independents. White Rabbit's product range now includes amazing ravioli, doughy focaccia bread and outrageously tasty ready meals.

Seven years later, the duo's mission is to create delicious Italian food for everyone to enjoy, no matter their needs, diet, or lifestyle. Per tutti – for everyone!

WHITE RABBIT
Free House
Freshly Made Food Served Daily
Stone Baked Artisan Pizza
white rabbit
white rabbit
white rabbit
SOURDOUGH
MARGHERITA
THE WHITE RABBIT
AWARD WINNING ALES
FRESHLY MADE
STONE BAKED PIZZA

The Rainbow Vegan Pizza

The Rainbow Vegan is a firm favourite of ours: a kaleidoscope of roasted vegetables marinated in harissa, on a bed of baby chard and cheese. We've used our own gluten-free bases, but feel free to make your own pizza dough!

Preparation time: 50 minutes | Cooking time: 30 minutes | Makes 2

4 tbsp harissa paste (our favourite is the Rose Harissa from Belazu)
1 White Rabbit Gluten-Free Base or your own homemade pizza base
50ml passata
1 yellow pepper
1 courgette
1 aubergine
Handful of baby chard or spinach
Handful of cheese (to make this pizza vegan, we'd recommend using MozzaRisella's vegan mozzarella)
Olive oil
Small handful of rocket

Preheat your oven to 180°c or 160°c fan or Gas Mark 4. First up, we are going to roast our veggies. Roughly chop all your veggies, discarding those tops and ends, making sure you deseed your pepper as well. Place in a baking tray and add your harissa – use extra if you want more of a kick! If it's a little thick, add a splash of water to ensure there's a good coating on your veggies. Pop them in the oven for 20 minutes.

After 20 minutes, take your vegetables out of the oven and set aside. Turn up your oven to 240°c or 220°c fan or Gas Mark 8.

Get your pizza bases and add a layer of that passata – the back of a spoon is the best way to do this. Scatter half of your harissa roasted veggies onto your pizza base, then sprinkle with the baby chard or spinach and finally your choice of cheese.

Place your pizza in the oven for up to 10 minutes. Cooking times could vary but with the oven being so hot we recommend keeping an eye on it.

Remove from the oven when the crust is golden and the cheese has melted. To serve, drizzle with olive oil and scatter rocket leaves on top. Repeat for the second pizza. Buon appetito!

From Farm to Fork

Dubbed one of Oxfordshire's 'best-kept secrets' by Ox In A Box, Worton Kitchen Garden offers food that's not just freshly prepared but freshly grown, in a beautifully rustic agricultural setting.

Worton Kitchen Garden is a restaurant and shop on a working farm, using regenerative practices to produce fantastic crops and livestock which are turned into delicious seasonal food. It was established around 15 years ago and has recently come under new ownership; Simon Spence joined the venture as a baker and progressed to chef before taking on Worton Kitchen Garden with the aim of becoming more sustainable and environmentally friendly.

The business has since moved to a no-dig form of regenerative farming, moving towards perennial instead of annual crops to further reduce the need to till the ground. This not only helps to produce fantastic and flavourful food, but also restores the soil and its biodiversity. Simon hopes they can show that giving back to the environment and making a difference is still a commercially viable way of farming. Even the resident farm animals do their part to keep the cycle going, with pedigree Saddleback pigs preparing the fields by digging up the perennial weeds and fertilising the soil, and the Indian runner ducks on slug patrol!

These sustainable crops – including fruit, vegetables, herbs and salad – and meat from the livestock are then turned into the delicious dishes offered in the restaurant at Worton Kitchen Garden. Menus vary according to the seasonal changes in their produce, and Simon draws inspiration from the travelling that was a big part of his former corporate life, one of the reasons he is committed to "redressing the balance" at Worton. Going forwards, the team are keen to build relationships with the local community, including Sobell House, and recently opened Coffee Shack on the Worton Estate, having partnered up with Ue Coffee Roasters in Witney to bring weekday treats to the locals.

Being set on a working farm, the surroundings at Worton Kitchen Garden are relaxed and rustic. There are various glass houses and polytunnels alongside the restaurant and shop, which are housed in converted barn buildings, all surrounded by a "beautiful madcap English cottage garden" to truly immerse customers in the farm environment. During the summer, tables are dotted throughout the gardens to create the feeling of dining in your own private idyll. Having started to gain some well-deserved recognition in local and national press, as well as being a Farmshop/Deli finalist in the 2021 Muddy Stilettos awards, Worton Kitchen Garden's success is no longer a secret!

Today's
Fresh Fish
IFE IS A MIRACLE
LIFE IS A MIRACLE

Nasu Dengaku

From the end of July, one of our key crops at the farm is beautiful purple aubergines - we sell lots in the shop and have to be resourceful in coming up with different recipes for the restaurant. One of our firm customer favourites is this simple Japanese dish.

Preparation time: 15 minutes | Cooking time: 60 minutes | Serves: 2 as a main course, 4 as a starter

For the aubergines
2 aubergines
100ml olive oil
Sesame seeds

For the sauce
200g white miso paste
100ml dashi
25ml sake
100g fresh ginger, grated and squeezed to release its juice

For the pickle
200g kohlrabi
100ml apple cider vinegar
2 dried chillies
1 tsp coriander seeds
1 tsp sugar
1 tsp salt

First, make the pickle. Here I have suggested kohlrabi, but you could use turnips, daikon, radishes, cucumbers or indeed carrots depending on what's to hand – just make sure it's a crisp, firm vegetable. Julienne your chosen vegetable so that each piece is a few millimetres wide. Next, put the vinegar and flavourings in a saucepan and bring to a simmer to dissolve the sugar and salt. Add the julienned vegetables and allow to cool.

Halve the aubergines lengthways through the stalk. Next, cut diagonal lines through each half in two directions to create a 'hedgehog' effect. The aim is to cut deeply to allow the sauce to permeate but without cutting through the skin.

Heat some of the olive oil until smoking hot in a flat pan. Place each aubergine half, cut side down, in the pan for a couple of minutes to brown the surface. Once all four pieces are browned, place them in an ovenproof dish browned side up, cover with foil and bake at 180°c for 30 minutes or until meltingly soft.

While the aubergine is baking, make the sauce by whisking together the miso, dashi, sake and ginger juice. Use a spoon to cover each piece of aubergine generously with sauce, making sure that the sauce goes down between all the cuts. Sprinkle with sesame seeds and place the whole thing under a hot grill until browned and sizzling.

To serve, arrange the aubergine pieces on cooked white rice and add a small mound of drained pickled vegetables to the side.

Dining with the Best Intentions

The Yurt at Nicholsons serves food with style underpinned by a deep-rooted commitment to the environment that has already garnered acclaim and support from the Michelin Guide and locals alike.

The Yurt at Nicholsons started life as a café on the site of a larger diverse business near North Aston, Oxfordshire, but has since become a destination restaurant for brunch and lunch in a stunning setting. As the name suggests, diners are seated within a yurt within the grounds of Nicholsons, a plant centre offering professional services on every aspect of plant care, landscaping, forestry and ecology. With such a strong connection to the natural environment, The Yurt is a restaurant with sustainability at its core and this ethos informs everything they do, from the food to the décor.

Andrew Carr, the head chef, has been overseeing the new direction of the restaurant since early 2022. Along with his sous chef David and front of house staff Chloe and Inga, the hardworking small team have made a name for The Yurt thanks to their modern British cookery and service that always brings a smile. The Michelin Guide recognised their achievements in summer 2022 by listing The Yurt as a new Inspector's Choice, and Andrew's next goal is to scoop a Michelin Green Star – something very few restaurants in the UK have done – in the near future.

The menus are heavily seasonal and often feature organic produce, about 40% of which is bought within the village including bread, fruit, dairy and of course vegetables grown on site in the Nicholsons nursery. In summer you might find dishes like tempura artichoke with a fricassee of the most abundant veg, desserts using Evesham strawberries and a parfait made with local dairy cream and foraged woodruff. Andrew enjoys taking classic dishes to the next level by adding his own twist and is always thinking about the local produce on offer, such as sausages made in-house with venison or pork sourced from nearby gamekeepers and farmers for his brunch menu.

"There's nowhere like Nicholsons that does what we do," says Andrew, "from composting and creating our own electricity on site to banning polystyrene and soon moving towards a fully electric fleet. Liz and Niel, the owners, are very forward thinking and sustainability is always the number one priority here." Not only evident in the delicious fresh food, customers can also see this approach the moment they walk into The Yurt: the weekly plant display at its centre and the custom-built recycled wood tables that fit the curve of the tent showcase how The Yurt is doing dining differently.

WELCOME TO
THE
YURT
@ NICHOLSONS
WE ARE OPEN TUESDAY TO SATURDAY
BRUNCH 9-11.45
LUNCH 12-2.30
WALK INS ARE MORE THAN WELCOME IF YOU WOULD
LIKE TO GUARANTEE YOUR SPACE, PLEASE BOOK VIA OUR

Twice Baked Cheese Soufflé with Granny Smith Apple, Toasted Hazelnut and Watercress Salad

An elegant, rich and indulgent dish that can be made a couple of days in advance, to make serving easier, and is guaranteed to impress, be it a dinner party or late night snack!

Preparation time: 30 minutes, plus 1 hour cooling | Cooking time: 30 minutes | Serves: 12

1 onion
1 bay leaf
4 cloves
700ml semi-skimmed milk
125g unsalted butter
125g plain flour
325g cheddar, grated
70g parmesan, grated
1 tsp English mustard
8 egg whites
5 egg yolks
Breadcrumbs

To serve

Double cream
Grated parmesan
Granny Smith apples
Toasted hazelnuts
Watercress
Balsamic vinegar

Stud the onion with the bay leaf and cloves, then place into a heavy-bottomed pan on a low heat along with the milk and leave to simmer for a couple of minutes. Strain the milk through a sieve, discarding the onion, and keep it warm.

In a separate pan, melt the butter and then stir in the flour to form a roux. Continuously stir over the heat until the mixture leaves the sides of the pan. Slowly add the hot milk in small batches, stirring all the time, until the mixture forms a thick béchamel sauce. Next, add the grated cheeses and mustard. Remove the pan from the heat and allow the sauce to cool to body temperature.

In a bowl, whisk the egg whites until they become thick; they should be able to hold themselves in the bowl when it's turned upside down. Add the yolks to the béchamel sauce, mix well, and then fold in the whisked egg white in batches until it's all combined.

Grease the pudding moulds with a little oil and then line them with a thin coating of breadcrumbs, to help you turn out the soufflés more easily. Pipe the soufflé mixture into each mould, then bake the soufflés in a bain-marie in the oven at 150°c for 20 minutes. Allow them to cool until slightly warm, at which point begin turning the soufflés out of the moulds onto a baking tray. Leave to finish cooling completely.

To serve

The soufflés are best eaten reheated (hence the twice baked in the name!) so they can be assembled accordingly once cool, or will last up to 3 days in the fridge before you want to serve them. Place the soufflés into an ovenproof serving dish, pour a little cream into the bottom and sprinkle over some more grated parmesan. Bake in a hot oven at 190°c for 8 minutes and serve straight away with a side salad of chopped apple, toasted hazelnuts and fresh watercress dressed in balsamic vinegar.

Directory

Acropolis Greek Taverna
146 London Road, Oxford OX3 9ED
01865766755
info@acropolisgreektaverna.uk
www.acropolisgreektaverna.uk
Instagram @acropolis_oxford
Facebook @acropolisoxford

Acropolis is devoted to bringing the best of Greece to your doorstep.

The Alice at The Randolph Hotel
Beaumont Street, Oxford OX1 2LN
01865 256400
www.thealiceoxford.com
hello@thealiceoxford.com
@thealiceoxford

An all-day dining room serving seasonal, locally sourced British dishes with a contemporary twist.

Bhoomi Kitchen
70 London Road, Headington
Oxford OX3 7PD
01865 762696
www.bhoomikitchen.co.uk
oxford@bhoomikitchen.co.uk
@bhoomikitchen_ and @bhoomirestaurant

South Indian food inspired by the state of Kerala, from traditional one pot curries to the famous Masala Dosa and Keralan style barbecue.

Café Coco
23 Cowley Road, Oxford OX4 1HP
01865 200232
www.cafecoco.co.uk
coco@cafecocogroup.com

Popular brunch and lunch spot with international food and great cocktails.

Café Tarifa
56-60 Cowley Road, Oxford OX4 1JB
01865 256091
www.cafetarifa.co.uk

A hidden oasis with an amazing space to host parties and private events.

The Eyston Arms
High Street, East Hendred, Wantage
Oxfordshire OX12 8JY
01235 833320
www.eystonarms.co.uk
info@eystonarms.co.uk
Facebook: Eyston Arms
Instagram @the.eyston.arms

Proper English pub with great food, service and atmosphere.

The Gardeners Arms
39 Plantation Road, Oxford OX2 6JE
01865 559814
www.thegardenersarms.co.uk
info@thegardenersarms.co.uk

Oxford's oldest serving 100% vegetarian and vegan kitchen, in a pub that regularly makes The Good Beer Guide and has the only turfed beer garden in Jericho.

Jolly Good Brownies
5 Mill Lane, East Hendred
Oxfordshire OX12 8JS
07917 542662
www.jollygoodbrownies.co.uk
@jollygoodbrownies

Jolly Good Brownies is a mail-order brownie company offering delicious gift wrapped brownies for all occasions.

Kazbar
25-27 Cowley Road, Oxford OX4 1JB
01865 202920
www.kazbar.co.uk

Tapas bar in a design-led space with handmade food and delicious cocktails.

The Old Bookbinders Ale House
17-18 Victor Street, Oxford OX2 6BT
01865 553549
www.oldbookbinders.co.uk
info@oldbookbinders.co.uk
Facebook: The Old Bookbinders
Instagram @oldbookbinders

Traditional pub specialising in bistro-style French food and real ales, at the heart of the community in Jericho.

Oxford Fine Dining Ltd
Unit 12, Oddington Grange, Weston on the Green
Oxon OX25 3QW
01865 728240
www.oxfordfinedining.co.uk
enquiries@oxfordfinedining.co.uk
Twitter: @OFDltd
Facebook: @OFDLtd
Instagram: @oxfordfinedining

Catering for weddings, events, dinners and fine dining banquets with innovation and creativity.

Parsonage Grill
1-3 Banbury Road, Oxford OX2 6NN
01865 292305
www.parsonagegrill.co.uk
info@parsonagegrill.co.uk
@ParsonageGrill

Parsonage Grill is famous for its intimate, bohemian, clubby atmosphere, where head chef Allan McLaughlin takes pride in creating classic British dishes with a modern, light touch.

The Picnic Hamper
37E Monument Park, Chalgrove
Oxford OX44 7RW
01865 891720
www.thepicnichamper.co.uk
info@thepicnichamper.co.uk
Facebook and Instagram @picnichamperchalgrove

Popular café and outside caterers serving hot food, salads, snacks and drinks with fresh ingredients, all cooked from scratch with consistent quality.

Pierre Victoire
9 Little Clarendon Street, Oxford OX1 2HP
01865316616
www.pierrevictoire.co.uk
pierrevictoire@hotmail.com
Facebook and Instagram @pierrevictoireoxford

Privately owned and family run for 26 years, this independent bistro offers fabulously cooked traditional French dishes at great prices, with a relaxed atmosphere reminiscent of Parisian cafés.

Pindy's Samosas Ltd
54 East Field Close, Headington OX3 7SH
07974 267620 / 07500 650151
www.pindys.com
Facebook @pindys.samosas and Instagram @pindys_samosas

Want delicious savoury or sweet delicacies delivered to your home, event or office? Look no further than Pindy's Samosas for parcelled up perfection.

The Plough at Hanney
Church Street, West Hanney OX12 0LN
01235 868987
www.theploughathanney.co.uk
enquiries@theploughathanney.co.uk

Community owned pub whose goal is to champion local farmers and local produce, as well as having a lot of fun along the way!

The Secret Supper Society
www.thesecretsuppersociety.com
Facebook: TheSecretSupperSociety
Instagram @secretsupper
Twitter @thesecretsupper

Self-taught cook Jules hosts a 'home from home' restaurant in the comfortable dining room of her farmhouse in North Oxfordshire, combining restaurant quality food with a relaxed dinner party atmosphere.

Studley Wood Golf Club
Horton-Cum-Studley, Oxford, Oxon OX33 1BF
01865 351122
office@studleywoodgolfclub.co.uk
www.studleywoodgolfclub.co.uk
@studleywoodgolfclub

Oxfordshire's hidden gem: more than a golf club, with relaxed and informal daytime dining. Come for coffee or a bite to eat in the beautiful surroundings of tranquil countryside.

Taste Tibet
109 Magdalen Road, Oxford OX4 1RQ
01865499318
www.tastetibet.com
hello@tastetibet.com
Facebook: /TasteTibetUK
Instagram and Twitter @TasteTibet

Taste Tibet is a restaurant and festival food stall based in Oxford. We serve the best momo dumplings and heartiest Himalayan curries this side of Everest!

The Tite Inn
Mill End, Chadlington
Oxfordshire OX7 3NY
015608 676910
www.thetiteinn.co.uk
enquiries@thetiteinn.co.uk
Instagram @titeinn

Stunning Cotswolds inn in a picturesque setting, with timeless décor and a welcoming personality. Our produce is fresh, local and seasonal and our ales are brewed less than a mile away with pure Chadlington spring water.

The White Hart
Fyfield, Abingdon
Oxfordshire OX13 5LW
01865 390585
www.whitehart-fyfield.com
Instagram: @thewhitehartfyfield
Twitter: @the_whitehart
Facebook: @whitehartfyfield

Award-winning 15th century dining pub with a passion for fresh seasonal produce and all things local.

The White Hart of Wytham
Wytham, Oxford OX2 8QA
01865 244372
info@whitehartwytham.com
www.whitehartwytham.com
Instagram @whitehartofwytham
Facebook and Twitter @WhiteHartWytham

Family and dog friendly pub with indoor and outdoor dining and bar areas; a hidden gem in the quintessentially English village of Wytham.

White Rabbit
www.whiterabbitpizza.co.uk
hello@whiterabbitpizza.co.uk
Instagram @white_rabbit_pizza_co

White Rabbit create gluten-free and plant-based Italian food. Available in a wide range of supermarkets including Sainsbury's, Waitrose and Morrisons.

Worton Kitchen Garden
Organic Farm Shop, Worton Rectory Farm
Cassington, Nr Oxford OX29 4SU
07710634 631
www.wortonkitchengarden.com
info@wkg.uk | @wortonkitchengarden

A magical oasis on the edge of Oxford comprising a smallholding, garden, farm shop and a hyper-seasonal farm to fork restaurant.

The Yurt at Nicholsons
The Park, North Aston, Bicester OX25 6HL
01869 340342 (Option 4)
www.nicholsonsgb.com/yurt/
theyurt@nicholsonsgb.com
Instagram @theyurtatnicholsons

A unique experience | food with style | sustainability in our hearts.

First edition printed in 2022 in the UK
ISBN: 978-1-910863-96-1
Special thanks to: Roger Allam, Matt Allwright, Paul Chahidi, Huw Edwards, Mel Giedroyc, Florence Pugh & Rick Stein
Written by: Katie Fisher and Lizzie Morton
Compiled by: Tim Wraith
Designed by: Phil Turner, Paul Cocker
Photography by: Paul Gregory
Additional pictures: John Cairns
Contributors: Lizzy Capps, Lis Ellis, Emma Toogood

Printed in Great Britain
by Bell and Bain Ltd, Glasgow

Published by Meze Publishing Limited
Unit 1b, 2 Kelham Square
Kelham Riverside
Sheffield S3 8SD
Web: www.mezepublishing.co.uk
Telephone: 0114 275 7709
Email: info@mezepublishing.co.uk

Sobell House
Churchill Hospital
Old Road
Headington
Oxford OX3 7LE
Web: www.sobellhouse.org
Telephone: 01865 225860
Email: mail@sobellhospice.org